ADVANCE PRAISE FOR

Vegans on Speciesism and Ableism: Ecoability Voices for Disability and Animal Justice

"This wonderfully insightful book challenges us to think more deeply and critically about social justice efforts, liberatory practices, and the intersectionality of people, animals, the environment. It's a must read for anyone committed to transformational social change."

—Dr. Jason Del Gandio, Co-editor, *Spontaneous Combustion: The Eros Effect and Global Revolution*

"Amidst the largest social uprising in our lifetime consideration for total liberation work is paramount to dismantling the interrelated ways racism, sexism, and classism work inextricably with ableism and speciesism. *Vegans on Speciesism and Ableism: Ecoability Voices for Disability and Animal Justice* edited by Anthony J. Nocella II and Amber E. George ignites readers to this collection action and invites us all to learn more about difference, diversity, and making real change."

—Dr. Johnny Lupinacci, Washington State University

"An urgent and necessary book that sheds light on the deeply entangled roots of violence and the oppression of humans with disability and the more-than-human world."

—Ângela Lamas Rodrigues, State University of Londrina, Brazil

"In the last ten years the ecoability movement has become a diverse and radical force for social justice, this book is necessary reading for scholars and activists who want to understand an ecoability framework which explores the intersections between disability, animal, environmental rights and liberation. The collection is a rallying cry against injustice, oppression and domination and for solidarity, mutual aid and total liberation."

—Dr. Will Boisseau, Director of Personnel, Institute of Critical Animal Studies

"*Vegans on Speciesism and Ableism* is a brilliant and powerful book bringing together disability and animal justice together. This beautiful thoughtful intersectional book pushes the boundaries of social justice in outstanding ways."

—Alisha Page, Director, Save the Kids

"As a neurodivergent activist who has struggled with having 'disabilities' all of their life, I've oftentimes felt isolated within social movements due to ableism and a lack of understanding around 'disabilities'. This book helps to bridge some of those gaps by challenging its readers to engage in direct change and to identify, critique, and deconstruct the ableist-speciesist connection."

—Jordan Halliday, Neurodivergent, Activist, Educator, and Former Social Movement Prisoner

"This book draws from and continues to push forward the aphorism that diversity is an absolutely crucial concept for ecological, biological, and social flourishing which should be celebrated. While contributors center on connections between disability, nonhuman animals, and the environment, no form of oppression or social justice is left out, setting an example for social justice advocates who are not fully inclusive."

—Nathan Poirier, Co-Director, Students for Critical Animal Studies

"A wonderful book co-edited by Anthony J. Nocella II and Amber E. George, *Vegans on Speciesism and Ableism* moves disability and animal justice forward in brilliant and critical ways. This is one of the most important books in the animal rights movement."

—Green Theory and Praxis Journal

"A powerful abolition pedagogy book that promotes total liberation and justice for all. This book edited by the outstanding scholar-activists Nocella and George is a must read for anyone working to end ableism and speciesism."

—Lucas Dietsche, Co-Editor, Transformative Justice Journal

"*Vegans on Speciesism and Ableism* edited by Nocella and George makes a particularly decisive and original contribution to the dynamic body/ies of literature that speak to critical animal studies, vegan praxis, intersectionality and total liberation. Crucially, the book has the potential to inspire new ways of understanding, thinking and being in the reader. In short it is a book that both demands to be read, *and* acted upon."

—Dr. Richard J. White, Sheffield Hallam University, UK

Vegans on Speciesism and Ableism

**RADICAL ANIMAL STUDIES
AND TOTAL LIBERATION**

Anthony J. Nocella II
Series Editor

Vol. 9

The Radical Animal Studies and Total Liberation series
is part of the Peter Lang Education list.
Every volume is peer reviewed and meets
the highest quality standards for content and production.

PETER LANG
New York • Bern • Berlin
Brussels • Vienna • Oxford • Warsaw

Vegans on Speciesism and Ableism

Ecoability Voices for Disability and Animal Justice

Edited by
Anthony J. Nocella II
and Amber E. George

PETER LANG

New York • Bern • Berlin
Brussels • Vienna • Oxford • Warsaw

Library of Congress Cataloging-in-Publication Control Number: 2021040918

Bibliographic information published by **Die Deutsche Nationalbibliothek**.
Die Deutsche Nationalbibliothek lists this publication in the "Deutsche
Nationalbibliografie"; detailed bibliographic data are available
on the Internet at http://dnb.d-nb.de/.

ISSN 2469-3065 (print)
ISSN 2469-3081 (online)
ISBN 978-1-4331-9288-3 (hardcover)
ISBN 978-1-4331-9009-4 (paperback)
ISBN 978-1-4331-9010-0 (ebook pdf)
ISBN 978-1-4331-9011-7 (epub)
DOI 10.3726/b18574

© 2022 Peter Lang Publishing, Inc., New York
80 Broad Street, 5th floor, New York, NY 10004
www.peterlang.com

Dedication

This book is dedicated to the family and friends of George Floyd and Breonna Taylor. This book demands justice for George Floyd and Breonna Taylor and the dismantling of the whole punitive justice system.

Table of Contents

Acknowledgments

We would like to thank everyone that is involved in the ecoability movement and field of study that is working to make the relationship between
disability, animal, and environmental liberation, advocacy, and justice. We
would like to thank the contributors of the book—Clifton Sanders, Lea
Lani Kinikini, S. Marek Muller, Daniel Salomon, Birkan Tas, Zoie (Zane)
McNeill, Rebecca Eli Long, T.N. Rowan, and Elisa Stone. We would like to
thank Peter Lang Publishing for believing in ecoability and publishing on
the movement. We would like to thank everyone at Peter Lang Publishing,
especially, Jackie Pavlovic, Patty Mulrane, and Dani Green from Peter Lang
Publishing. We would like to thank all of those who wrote reviews for the
book: Peace Studies Journal, Transformative Justice Journal, Green Theory
and Praxis Journal, Richard White, Jason Del Gandio, Nathan Poirier,
Jordan Halliday, Will Boisseau, Alisha Page, Johnny Lupinacci, and Ângela
Lamas Rodrigues. We would like to thank Institute for Critical Animal
Studies, Critical Animal Studies Academy, Critical Animal Studies Society,
Ecoability Collective, Academy for Peace Education, Salt Lake Community
College's Department of Criminal Justice, Faculty Senate, JEDI4ST research
center, Utah Reintegration Project, JEDI Hub, JEDI Senate, Utah Vegan
Runners, Arissa Media Group, Wisdom Behind the Walls, Poetry Behind the
Walls, Hangar 15 Bicycles, Galen College, Academy for Peace Education, AK
Press, Syracuse Quaker Meeting, Alternatives to Violence Project, Outdoor
Empowerment, Lowrider Studies Journal, Punk Studies Journal, Journal of
Hip Hop Studies, International Hip Hop Studies Association, Institute for
Hip Hop Activism, Lowrider Studies, and Total Liberation Campaigns.

Foreword

CLIFTON SANDERS

Although it has only existed as a category of inquiry and discourse for a decade, the ecoability movement has produced a remarkably complex and diverse body of work to-date, including critical studies, monographs, conferences, and commentary that break new ground with each publication. Perhaps I should not be so surprised by this, inasmuch as ecoability emerged out of recognitions and relationships that are best described as *intersectional.* In this book, Anthony Nocella and Amber George assemble scholar-activists to probe the confluences between veganism, critical animal studies, disability, animal, environmental rights, and so on. Formulating the ecoability paradigm creates new space for an activist agenda that critically explores a new universe of connections in ways which illuminate even more complex interdependencies. This in turn further motivates collaboration, support, activism, and, ultimately, desires for justice realized via the total liberation of all species and nature-self.

As a newcomer to ecoability scholarship, I find this book personally compelling in several ways. I have been a teacher and academic administrator at Salt Lake Community College for more than 25 years, but my formal professional training and prior work experience was as a doctorate organic chemist and research scientist. My undergraduate years and summer research internships in industry occurred during the same time frame as the widespread publication of chemical assaults upon the natural world such as the Love Canal disaster and other high-profile pollution and ecosystem destruction scenarios, along with the devastating economic and human impacts of environmental racism upon marginalized and oppressed communities. Moreover, I grew up in Turners Station, Maryland, a working class African American community in southeastern Baltimore County. Turners Station is situated on Bear Creek (a tributary of the Chesapeake Bay) across the water from Sparrows Point, where steel mills, shipyards and power plants thrived from World War II until the 1970s and were notorious for frequent fish kills, toxic ponds, and heavy metal ground contamination, some of which still exist in and around my childhood community. (I note, extreme scientific caution notwithstanding, that Henrietta Lacks, whose HeLa cancer cells are celebrated worldwide by the medical community but only recently afforded her recognition, lived in Turners Station at the time of her cervical cancer diagnosis.)

After graduate school, my professional research in biomaterials technology also brought me in contact with animal testing of candidate materials for medical devices intended to improve human health and well-being. And, because of dear friends who are differently abled, I served for several years as a citizen-advocate for a disability rights organization. The point of these biographical snippets is to admit that Anthony Nocella's invitation to me to write this forward has, through reading and studying the book chapters, moved me into a new space of deep recollection, mourning, reflection, and conviction via an ecoability lens. Several (perhaps all) authors in this book in some way honor their experiential journey through their articles. It is very obvious to me that these scholarly works are also deeply personal and forward-looking responses to various kinds of violence and marginalizations experienced first-hand. I find T.N. Rowan's chapter on interspecies trauma remarkably heartfelt and incisive. Although I do not cite all the authors of the book in this Foreword, please know that I am overwhelmingly grateful that all these courageous voices accepted the opportunity to speak and reinforce each other in this space. Taken altogether, this collection conveys a prophetic witness that bequeaths dignity, force, urgency, and moral imagination to a strident call to sacrificial, liberatory action. I believe that this witness provides a rich template and guide for ecoability novices like myself to deconstruct our own experiences and cherished myths in pursuit of an activist lifestyle. For example, Zoe (Zane) McNeill and Rebecca Eli Long's chapter inspires consonances between the plights of Duplin County, North Carolina, and Turners Station, Maryland. They enable me to perceive a shared narrative of exploitation, marginalization, racism, ableism, and ecological destruction, despite the temporal distance of their respective events. Both situations exhibit sadly what we have known for millennia—that exploitation and brute material excess destabilizes, disrupts, and eventually destroys complex (eco) systems. Writ large, the tragic costs of ignoring intersectionality and interdependency championed in the ecoability frame render inevitable the end of the broad road to planetary destruction.

Two chapters, by S. Marek Muller and Daniel Salomon, respectively, address conflict within and between various ecoability standpoints. These scholars employ a variety of innovative critical approaches to deconstruct and analyze the sources of conflict. These analyses reveal fresh paradigms for connecting and reframing opposition within a total liberation context. For example, Muller uses rhetorical criticism to evaluate the scientific controversies and eco-ableist arguments deployed in PETA's 'Got Autism' campaign. Muller also articulates analogies between species oppression and ableist oppression and finds a way forward free of cynical, manufactured ableist-speciesist dichotomy. Likewise, Salomon's chapter offers an approach to ecoability equity/animal equity conflict resolutions which incorporates multiple social justice methods informed from liberal arts and other perspectives. Birken Tas's chapter brilliantly demonstrates how critical analysis of animal breeding easily draws connections to studies about scientific racism, veganism, speciesism, and disability.

In bringing my remarks to a close, I hope that this book not only meets the needs of ecoability scholars and activists but also reaches beyond the scholarly vanguard to engage and captivate seeker audiences of all types. The writings assembled under the theme of this book open new vistas with great success, demonstrating novel and unprecedented interdependencies between concepts, theory, and praxis that might appear disparate at first glance. Such innovative syntheses, teased out superbly by each writer, illustrate the astounding power of the ecoability paradigm to catalyze complex, nuanced, deep critical discourse, which clarifies, inspires, and critiques activism for total liberation. With deep humility, appreciation, and enthusiasm, I commend this book.

Preface

Lea Lani Kinikini

Speciesism, or the assumption of human superiority leading to the exploitation of nonhuman animals, plants, airways, waterways, ecosystems, and minerals, is a prism that refracts the multiple ways in which human beings exploit each other, through normative paradigms that argue a teleological bent to human history that sees able-bodied, often male, always "white" or a master race—as the *denouement* or final point of all existence: that when "doomsday" comes, there will be a *"last* [able-bodied] *man standing."* Ecological disaster is human disaster. Humans are disastrous to ecosystems. Without intervention, this planet, our blue planet, will die in the coming epoch. It has already begun. Coral reefs, as a being—a collective being—through which the planet breathes, is and has been for the past decades literally dying—so are our rivers and waterways, soils, skies, and the animal life. Even as we write, the Covid-19 pandemic compounds social traumas resulting in death worlds visiting marginalized peoples particularly urban Black and Brown and native and indigenous rural peoples on reservations, far more than those affluent "conquerors." How does one think beyond dominance of body, of human centric speciesism, and of violent incurring of one over an "other?" Ecoability provides some answers, beginnings, and continuances of critical thought about why and when should we re-think environmental justice through disability discourses of the body and dominance.

While the surveillance and privacy rights debates brought on by the 2020 pandemic resets human thinking to be more open to governmental, public health and technocratic controls, a small field known as "ecoability" captures the fringe of speciesism, a coral reef fringing a sunken volcanic mountain. Ecoability, founded in 2010 by Anthony J. Nocella II, is an intersectional eddy (a circular movement of water, counter to a main current, causing a small whirlpool) within the environmental justice movement that runs counter enough to increase our imagination of looking beyond the limits of environmental justice. The field argues we must include those with mental and physical disabilities into the dialogue, who have been for too long silenced and marginalized. We have found through the rise in sales of outdoor gear that people in the U.S. are going to nature for sanctuary and therapy during the Covid-19 pandemic. It is not shocking that if we eat organic and vegan we will contract and carry less diseases. It is not shocking that if we dovetail disability discourse into environmental justice that we come up with a liberating if obvious conclusion: that life is critically dependent on diversity. The deep ethical caverns that ecoability as a field opens up, for theory and for innovating educational praxis and pedagogy, have never been more urgent.

As an example, the necessity to add theoretical tracks to environmental justice is to see the animation of nature allows us view legal rights that nature holds has by virtue of nature bearing a spirit, possessing mana, or potentiality for being/becoming to Native and indigenous Oceanian (Pacific) philosophy and worldview which sees animals, trees, plants, land, soil, rocks, winds, rains, and ocean waves as animate, as *beings* invested with mana (power) capable and holding agentic power to cause effect—often causing harm should humans abuse or misuse. Think about our relatedness to nature inscribed in Native cultures on Turtle Island—that "totem" that connects me to my tribe, also connects me to my genealogy of my brother the kalo (taro) plant, my ancestor the seaweed, and my guides the winds, waves, birds, sharks, whales, and dolphins, amongst others. The "tapu" system, one of the ritual controls to ensure persistence, sustainability, and recovery, came to define the cultural "kastoms" of Oceanic peoples, ensures that humans do not overstep their limits, throwing the ecosystem into crisis.

Anti-racist and anti-ableist politics underscores this field. The field connects many threads and weaves them into the opening: that all beings are created *to be*; that "nature's way" is diversity and interdependency; that human thought, philosophy, and human domination are destruction. That until we see our brother the bear, our father the eagle, our mother the ocean, that until we liberate our thinking away from dogma that tells us because we walk upright, because we "can" dominate does not—never has—mean we should: to do so ensures peril and irreparable destruction. Or the knowledge that interdependency and relationality has human survival dependent on being subservient to not dominant over nature. Bob Marley channeled this best when he sang Lee Scratch Perry's "Duppy Conqueror." Duppy is a disembodied spirit originating in Central Africa. The duppy is part of Bantu folklore. A duppy can be either the manifestation (in human or animal form) of the soul of a dead person or a malevolent supernatural being. To acknowledge spirit flows through all—and that human agents can reverse trends—is important work.

This book by Anthony J. Nocella II and Amber E. George is an outstanding collaborative project bringing diverse voices together for total liberation, while centering nonhuman animals, the Earth, and those with disabilities. To protect the planet from capitalism and other forms of environmental exploitation and destruction, the answer is simple: We must come together and value different as does any healthy ecosystem. We cannot define or claim that humans are the most important and powerful species, but rather humble ourselves next to keynote species such as the bee and worm. Colonialism has not only oppressed and killed many humans but has also wiped of the planet thousands of species never to be seen again for the reason of domination. This book is not about just being read but about being used to ignite a rage in all of us to defend the sacred (the Earth) by any means necessary including changing how we live, eat, travel, work, and breed.

Pick up this book. Think about this field. Look about at the animate reefs, oceans, mountains, animals, our relations. That until we recognize, that until ALL are free—includes rivers, lakes, mountain ranges, sky, wind and cloud, rain, sea, and all nonhuman animals—and until we see that not we but they are going to be here long after "us," we must continue to mitigate against our worst self—our greedy, egoist, dominating, and conquering "duppy" selves. Until western culture eschews the foundation of self-righteousness that divine granted human dominion, a divine that required human and nonhuman animals sacrifice, without checking the worst parts of our selves: our fixation with a teleological myth in human progress, we must resist and dismantle this among us or we will be doomed.

Introduction: Getting in the Outdoors with Disabilities: Fun, Collaboration, and Total Liberation

ANTHONY J. NOCELLA II AND AMBER E. GEORGE

Introduction

The ecoability movement founded in 2010 emerged from critical animal studies (Best, Nocella II, Kahn, Gigliotti, & Kemmerer, 2007; Nocella II, Sorenson, Socha, & Matsuoko, 2014), and the Institute for Critical Animal Studies (n.d.) has come a long way with many people writing and engaging with disability, animal, environmental rights, justice, advocacy, and liberation. Ecoability was founded by Anthony J. Nocella II, Judy K.C. Bentley, and Janet Duncan with the first book published in 2012 (Nocella II, Bentley, & Duncan, 2012). It is now an international field and movement with over a dozen books published and several academic conferences on the topic (Nocella II, George, & Schatz, 2014). Using various conceptions of anti-capitalism, anti-fascism, anti-oppression, and anti-domination theory, ecoability explores how ecological destruction intersects with nonhuman animal and disability oppression (Nocella II & George, 2019). The goal is to create spaces where people with disabilities, nature, and nonhuman animals are supported for inter-dependency, collaboration, mutual aid, direct democracy, and value difference for all (Nocella II et al., 2019).

People with mental and physical disabilities have discovered brilliant methods of connecting with nature such as, but not limited to, skiing, biking, windsurfing, boating, climbing, scuba diving, trail running, bird watching, camping, hiking, rafting, kayaking, triathlons, surfing, ski diving, and paragliding. These activities have helped people with disabilities relate to their disabilities in new holistic ways. Many nonprofits provide access to nature for people with disabilities. The two types of nonprofits that assist people with disabilities to explore nature are (1) therapeutic based and (2) recreational.

Both are important and can foster veganism, animal advocacy, and environmental protection. Under an ecoability framework, these connections with nature demonstrate how people with disabilities rally against violent medical practices, pathologization, and institutionalization (Nocella II, 2012).

While many nonprofits support the inclusion of people with disabilities into integrated outdoor programs, some still segregate the most severely disabled individuals away from mainstream society. It is assumed that the presence of someone with a developmental disability may hamper the ecological learning gains of nondisabled children. However, no study has demonstrated that segregating children according to their disability positively benefits either group in building a relationship with nature or each other. The results of one particular study demonstrated that both the students with and those without disabilities enjoyed learning about nature together and formed valuable relationships based on their shared ecological experience (Schleien et al., 1994).

The curriculums designed to teach people with disabilities about sustainability, environmental problems, and ecological responsibility are few and far between (Nocella II, Drew, George, Ketenci, Lupinacci, Purdy, & Schatz, 2019). Several studies have proven that this learning approach has not been adopted in special education classrooms in an inclusive format (Stone, 2007). All students must have the opportunity to learn about the interconnections and dependencies we share with species and Earth's entities. Special education programs typically address environmental concerns only through gardening programs (Haines & Kilpatrick, 2007). While learning about plant life cycles and connecting their bodies with the soil is impactful, it is simply not enough. This includes understanding how being a consumer under capitalism threatens our environment and exploits nonhuman animals, how to advocate for those who have been marginalized, including the self, establishing eco-friendly habits and developing other ways to sustain all types of life on this planet (Best & Nocella II, 2004; Best & Nocella II, 2006). These values should be taught throughout the school year, not just during an isolated unit of learning about gardening (Kahn, 2010).

There are many nonprofits with a mission to introduce people with disabilities to nature through outdoor sports such as climbing, rafting, biking, and scuba diving, but many do not discuss environmental protection, sustainability, and animal advocacy. They stay away from social responsibility, because they think that if they discuss it with their clients and the public they will lose track of their mission and lose clients. Ecoability disagrees completely and argues for social responsibility, and discussing the philosophical similarity between disability and nature, where everything is different, interdependent, and diverse, is the foundation of a healthy ecosystem. Thus, every nonprofit that introduces humans to nature must promote ecological sustainability and animal advocacy (Singer, 1975; Regan, 1983).

Humans who get involved in nature have a greater chance of being advocates for nature. However, when there are steep physical barriers to keep certain people from enjoying nature, we risk missing people to join our cause. We are not advocating for cementing the Grand Canyon or the local hiking paths, but rather wish to have more inclusion and accessibility. For instance, since bike shops are eager to sell able-bodied bicycles that costs thousands of dollars, why not also stock affordable off-road wheelchairs? Or perhaps the local sporting goods store could sell adaptable climbing harnesses for those that have physical disabilities. There is significant work needed to make nature-based activities more inclusive of Black Indigenous People of Color (BIPOC), people with disabilities, LGBTTQQIA+ people, and people of lower income, youth, and women.

Corporations and nonprofit service-based organizations are both involved in being more inclusive of nature-based activities, but they both profit from the inclusion of those mentioned nature-based activities. The group that is lacking in inclusionary efforts is the activist community. Generally, the activist community is concerned with ending the human impact on nature and not introducing humans to nature. If humans want to save the planet, we must encourage everyone, and not just the privileged few, to have a healthy, sustainable relationship with nature.

This book aims to unify disability activists with animal and environmental activists to defend that marginalized people have the ability, interest, and right to build a healthy and sustainable relationship with nature. We must develop these relationships; it is life or death of the planet. Until people understand how we are truly dependent on the planet for everything including our lives, we will continue to kill the planet and thus ourselves.

This book is also about protecting nonhuman animals from being tested on, exploited for human entertainment, consumed for food and clothing, and killed for human development. The contributors in this volume call for readers to adopt conscious, sustainable veganism. Veganism is not only about ending the oppression of nonhuman animals but also ending all oppression. We need to reclaim veganism as a sociopolitical identity and not one that corporations get to define, capitalize on, and co-op as if it were their own.

The key to building a healthy and sustainable relationship with nature requires that you be an ecological minimalist when it comes to buying and using equipment to engage with nature (Kemmerer & Nocella II, 2011). For instance, instead of purchasing brand new gear, why not recycle and reuse previously owned equipment? Corporations are showing different identities in their marketing, but can that marketing become a reality, where society does our part in welcoming ALL people to nature?

This collection starts with S. Marek Muller's timely chapter "Got Autism?: PETA and the Rhetoric of Eco-Ableism." This analysis suggests that total liberation can be achieved by harnessing the power of language and argumentation to empower animal rights scholars and activists. The second essay written by Daniel Salomon, "Getting to Solidarity: Toward an Interest-Based Conflict Resolution Approach to Resolving the Conflict between Ecoability Equity and Animal Equity," provides critical commentary on inclusion for neurodiversity within ecoability communities. Chapter 3 is written by Birkan Taş, "Selection *for* and *against* Disability: Assistance Dogs," to discuss the issues surrounding dependency, dog breeding, and use of dogs for assisting people with disabilities. Chapter 4, "Queering the Animate Body: Toxicity, Ecoability, and Multispecies Solidarity in Duplin County, North Carolina," written by Zoie (Zane) McNeill and Rebecca Eli Long explores how toxicity has impacted marginalized communities, including human, nonhuman, and environmental entities. And finally, the last chapter to round out this collection is written by T. N. Rowan, entitled, "Trauma-Informed Activism: New Directions for Interspecies Trauma in Ecoability and Critical Animal Studies." Rowan's chapter provides useful practices for supporting vegans, scholars, and activists with Secondary-Traumatic Stress Disorder (STSD).

Conclusion: How to Collaborate on Book Projects

Editing a book is a collaborative mutual aid activity praised by critical disability studies and ecoability. We (Amber E. George and Anthony J. Nocella II) have had a few horrible experiences editing with people. For this reason, the conclusion of this Introduction is unorthodox but useful. We have found that book projects flounder for some of the following reasons:

1. People have horrible or no communication.
2. People do not have the skills they claimed to have.
3. People expect to do less because of their identity or position such as being the boss, senior scholar, title at a prestigious university, parent, age, experience, multiple jobs, paid less, or simply just busy.
4. People have different politics.
5. People do not respect deadlines.
6. People pay others to do their part of the project.
7. People ignore all communication.

8. People give up on the project but still want the credit.
9. People lie to those involved in the book and the publisher on workload.
10. People have abusive personal relationships or relationships that end.

This book is the seventh book that we (Amber E. George and Anthony J. Nocella II) have written together. We have a healthy, impactful, working relationship and feel we can share some pointers on how to collaborate on a book project successfully:

1. Communicate regularly.
2. Be forthcoming about your abilities, responsibilities, and desire to pursue the project.
3. Be respectful and trustworthy; be a leader and a follower.
4. Periodically assess the distribution of labor.
5. Honor each other's strengths and weaknesses.
6. Familiarize yourself with what parts of the project the other likes to do.
7. Know what is required for the project.
8. Assess when to pick up your colleague's load, while requesting the load be evened out later in the project.
9. Be fair when the workload is uneven, necessitating a departure from the project.
10. Develop a strong working relationship with the publication staff so that should a problem arise, you have an ally to assist you.

We hope this conclusion has helped you. Remember why you write and collaborate with people. It should not be about working with someone famous or working with someone you can exploit. It is about having a mutual and collaborative relationship, where both benefit for the sake of an important project to share to the world that promotes total liberation (Pellow, 2014). We ground our collaborative efforts in mutual aid and anarchism, which is nonauthoritarian, anti-oppressive, liberatory, punitive abolition, and anti-dominating (Shannon, Nocella II, & Asimakopoulos, 2012; Nocella II, Seis, & Shantz, 2020).

To create justice, equity, liberation, and inclusion in the world, there are three simple broad steps we refer to as the 3Ds—disrupt, discuss, and dismantle. One must first *disrupt* through escalation tactics by activists such as protesting, boycotts, lockdowns, lie-ins, sit-ins, rallies, banner drops, hunger-strikes, fasts, blockades, monkeywrenching, and direct action (Del Gandio,

& Nocella II, 2014). After enough disruption community organizers facilitate *discussions* with families, friends, organizations, countries, institutions, and companies in mediations, negotiations, arbitrations, community circles, brainstorms, workshops, teach-ins, lectures, and other educational forums that share knowledge to end ignorance and hate. Finally, after education and knowledge is shared to develop the tipping-point where there are enough people supporting the cause in society, *dismantling* of the social problem through revolution is possible.

References

Best, S., & Nocella II, A. J. (2004). *Terrorists or freedom fighters?: Reflections on the liberation of animals.* New York, NY: Lantern Books.

Best, S., & Nocella II, A. J. (2006). *Igniting a revolution: Voices in defense of the Earth.* Oakland, CA: AK Press.

Best, S., Nocella II, A. J., Kahn, R., Gigliotti, C., & Kemmerer, L. (2007). Introducing critical animal studies. *Journal of Critical Animal Studies, 5*(1), 4–5.

Del Gandio, J., & Nocella II, A. J. (2014). *Educating for action: Strategies to ignite social justice.* Gabriola Island, BC CA: New Society Publishers.

Haines, S., & Kilpatrick, C. (2007). Environmental education saves the day: Becoming a project learning tree (plt)-certified school unified faculty, boosted student achievement, and saved one school from closure. *Science and Children, 44*(8), 42–47.

Institute for Critical Animal Studies (n.d.). *About ICAS: History.* Retrieved on July 17, 2011 from http://www.criticalanimalstudies.org/about/

Kahn, R. (2010). *Critical pedagogy, ecoliteracy, & planetary crisis: The ecopedagogy movement.* New York, NY: Peter Lang.

Kemmerer, L., & Nocella II, A. J., (2011). *Call to compassion: Religious perspectives on animal advocacy.* New York, NY: Lantern Books.

Nocella II., A., J., Bentley, K. C., & Duncan, J. M. (2012). *Earth, animal, and disability liberation: The rise of the eco-ability movement.* New York, NY: Peter Lang.

Nocella II, A. J., Drew, C., George, A. E., Ketenci, S., Lupinacci, J., Purdy, I., & Schatz, J. L. (2019). *Education for total liberation: Critical animal pedagogy and teaching against speciesism.* New York, NY: Peter Lang.

Nocella II, A. J., & George, A. E. (2019). *Intersectionality of critical animal studies: A historical collection.* New York, NY: Peter Lang.

Nocella II., A. J., George, A. E., & Lupinacci, J. (2019). *Animals, disability, and the end of capitalism.* New York, NY: Peter Lang.

Nocella II., A. J., George, A. E., & Schatz, J. L. (2014). *The intersectionality of critical animal, disability, and environmental studies: Toward eco-ability, justice, and liberation.* New York, NY: Lexington Books.

Nocella II, A. J., Seis, M., & Shantz, J. (2020). *Classic writings in anarchist criminology: A historical dismantling of punishment and domination.* Oakland, CA: AK Press.

Nocella II, A. J., Sorenson, J., Socha, K., & Matsuoka, A. (2014). *Defining critical animal studies: An intersectional social justice approach for liberation.* New York, NY: Peter Lang.

Pellow, D. (2014). *Total liberation: The power and promise of animal rights and the radical Earth liberation movement.* Minneapolis, MN: University of Minnesota Press.

Regan, T. (1983). *The case for animal rights.* Los Angeles, CA: University of California Press.

Schleien, S., Hornfeldt, D., & McAvoy, L. (1994). Integration and environmental/outdoor education: The impact of integrating students with severe developmental disabilities on the academic performance of peers without disabilities. *Therapeutic Recreation Journal, 28*(1), 25–34.

Shannon, D., Nocella, A. J., II, & Asimakopoulos, J. (2012). The accumulation of freedom: Writings on Anarchist economics. Oakland, CA: AK Press.

Singer, P. (1975). *Animal liberation.* New York, NY: Ecco.

Stone, M. (2010). A schooling for sustainability framework. *Teacher Education Quarterly, 37*(4), 33–46.

1. Got Autism?: PETA and the Rhetoric of Eco-Ableism

S. Marek Muller

Introduction

Upon reading the title of this chapter, I imagine readers thinking: "What did PETA do *this* time?" In this chapter, I assess the rhetorical insufficiencies and ethical incoherencies of People for the Ethical Treatment of Animals' (PETA) much reviled "Got Autism?" campaign. Specifically, I assess the argumentative foundations of the campaign in which PETA suggested a causal connection between the consumption of dairy products and autism/autistic behaviors.

PETA, an animal rights organization founded in 1980 by current president Ingrid Newkirk, is infamous for its provocative and at times offensive animal rights campaigns. From nude protest to drenching bystanders in fake blood, a simple Google search is all it takes to understand PETA's general rhetorical strategy: Any publicity is good publicity. The organization is respected and reviled within animal liberation communities, with some praising activists' willingness to do anything and everything to promote a vegan lifestyle and others condemning the organization's tendency to appropriate the struggles of marginalized communities for their own benefit. Whether one loves or hates PETA, the organization remains one of the most well-funded and well-known animal rights organizations in the world. Given their intense political, social, and economic capital, I offer critical animal studies scholars and animal rights activists an opportunity to examine PETA's discursive strategies and tactics and assess its implications for "total liberation" (Best, 2014).

Critical animal studies is a theory-to-activist approach to scholarship that disavows theory for theory's sake. Taking nonhuman animal oppression as its primary focus, the field identifies the use and abuse of nonhuman animal life for humans' instrumental ends to be an atrocity in need of immediate resolution. However, it denounces single issue campaigns and instead situates speciesist oppression within interconnected matrices of exploitation including ableism. Arguing that nonhuman animals will not be free until humans are also free (and vice versa), the field and its followers adhere to an ethic of total liberation (Best, 2009). In this chapter, I merge critical animal studies' commitment to nonhuman animal liberation within another prescriptive field of study: critical rhetoric. I advocate for total liberation by focusing on the constitutive power of language and persuasion. PETA's "Got Autism?" campaign is not only a case study of eco-ableist activism within animal rights communities but also an exemplar of how studying the building blocks of argumentation can assist animal rights scholars and activists in their quest for the total liberation of species.

Critiquing PETA may seem to be an all-too-obvious (and perhaps all-too-meaningless) exercise. The organization's primary communication strategy is to invite moral shocks in their audiences through shocking or inflammatory texts or performances (Matusitz & Forrester, 2013). They do so because intensified media coverage of the organization could potentially bring the issue of animal rights further into the public eye. As such, they have been accused of racism, sexism, fatphobia, and ableism on more than one occasion and will likely not change their marketing strategy anytime soon. I argue, however, that studying PETA's "Got Autism" campaign through a critical rhetorical lens affords animal liberation scholars and activists a unique opportunity to identify and deconstruct the ableist-speciesist nexus. In doing so, we might create meaningful revisions and reinventions of animal liberation campaigns that are not only rhetorically powerful but also helpful in keeping with an ethic of total liberation.

As an autistic person, a total liberationist vegan, and an academic practitioner of "critical rhetoric," I use this chapter to explain the value of engaging in not only "critiques of domination" (assessing how privileged groups oppress the marginalized) but also "critiques of freedom" (assessing how freedom-fighting groups need to do better in the service of securing freedom for others). Through my rhetorical criticism I posit that PETA's campaign is counterproductive to an ethic of total liberation for the following reasons: (1) In creating this controversy, PETA employs a rhetoric of eco-ableism; (2) PETA unethically misrepresents scientific data on autism by creating a manufactured scientific controversy; and (3) In dehumanizing autistic humans to humanize nonhuman animals, PETA misses a valuable opportunity to rhetorically manifest the interconnected plights of autistic humans and nonhuman animals where they are marginalized, harmed, and killed in an ableist-speciesist landscape.

Context

In 2008, residents of Newark, New Jersey went for an everyday drive by the downtown Prudential Center only to be confronted with a disturbing new billboard. On the billboard was the image of a bowl of cereal—specifically of cheerios in milk. The cheerios had formed the shape of a frowning face. To the right of the sad cereal was black text over a blue background. In a play on the dairy industry's famous "Got Milk?" advertising campaign from the 1990s, this billboard's text read: "Got Autism?" In smaller text was the claim: "Studies have shown a link between cow's milk and autism. Find out more at GoVeg.com" (see image 1).

The billboard received local and nationwide news coverage. PETA explained that it chose Newark because the area had a large population of autistic children (Salahi, 2008). It planned to place more billboards in other cities where autism was most prevalent. According to Vice President Bruce Friedrich, the rationale behind the billboard was "to let the parents of autistic children know that they very well may see an improvement in their child's symptoms if they remove dairy" (qtd. in Salahi, 2008, para. 12). Despite calls from individuals and autistic advocacy organizations to remove the billboard, PETA did not budge. Instead, the billboard company itself pulled the image from distribution, no longer wishing to be associated with the controversy.

Although the billboard was discontinued, the "Got Autism?" campaign continued digitally. Currently, if one types "dairy" and "autism" into a Google search, PETA's website is either the first or one of the first results to show up, often surrounded by a series of other websites that mention the PETA campaign. While the image of the frowning bowl of cereal was recently removed from digital distribution, the webpage subtitled "Learn about the links between dairy and the disorder" argues that "scientific studies have shown that many autistic kids improve dramatically when put on a diet free of dairy products" (PETA, n.d., para. 2). Central to the website's argument are hyperlinks to two studies conducted by the University of Rome supposedly showing a connection between dairy consumption and autistic behavior as well as a mother's narrative: "There was nothing to lose, so I decided to eliminate all the dairy products from his diet. What happened next was nothing short of miraculous. Miles stopped screaming, he didn't spend as much time repeating actions, and, for the first time in months, he let his sister hold his hands to sing "Ring around a Rosy" (PETA, n.d., para. 5).

From 2008 to now, the "Got Autism" campaign has caused extreme offense among autistic people and those who care about them. Ari Ne'eman of the Autistic Self Advocacy Network put forth a petition urging PETA to remove the offensive ad. The petition, which garnered over 1,000 signatures, stated, "By exploiting us, PETA becomes a culprit in the social forces that marginalize people with disabilities and lead to the discrimination and prejudice that truly disable us" (Ne'eman, 2008a, para. 1). *Gizmodo* reported, "This is the most cynical, horrifying thing I've heard in ages" (Anders, 2014, para. 1). Some doctors were less concerned for the impact on autistic persons than they were for uninformed allistic people. Dr. Susan McGrew, associate professor of pediatrics at Vanderbilt University, claimed, "They will be scared that they'll get autism if they drink milk" (qtd. in Salahi, 2008, para. 4–5).

Despite unending criticisms on factual and ethical grounds, PETA seems disinterested in deleting its "Got Autism" campaign from the internet. Defending the original billboard, Friedrich mocked, "It's kind of funny to imagine how anybody in the autistic support community could take issue with a campaign that educates people to help autism" (qtd. in Salahi, 2008, para. 14). When the campaign's main webpage gained media attention again in 2014, PETA's Executive Vice President Tracy Reiman claimed: PETA's website provides parents with the potentially valuable information that researchers have backed up many families' findings that a dairy-free diet can help kids with autism...Cow's milk might be the perfect food for baby cows, but it might also be making kids sick. (Anders, 2014, ptd. qtd. para 8). The same thing occurred in 2017, when a PETA spokesman responded to Twitter critiques of the campaign by telling *The Mighty*: "Many families have found that a dairy-free diet can help children with autism" (qtd. in Davidson, 2017, para. 6). To this day, PETA has not apologized for its "Got Autism?" campaign. And if PETA continues to be PETA, it probably never will.

Critical Rhetoric for Total Liberation

I am a rhetorician by profession. Whereas the term "rhetoric" is often used as a pejorative to describe artful and deceptive language, the actual meaning and study of rhetoric is quite different. Most simply, rhetoric can be understood as the study of arguments. Rhetorical studies most typically examine persuasion (communication from one party resulting in attitudinal or behavioral change in another party) as a mode of discourse. The purpose of studying rhetoric is to (1) learn the most effective modes of persuasion in response to specific exigences in order to (2) become a more *effective* and *ethical* participant in civic life. I posit that viewing PETA's "Got Autism" campaign through the lens of rhetorical studies—specifically *critical* rhetorical studies—offers animal liberationists keen insights into why certain arguments for animal rights succeed, some fail, and some can be reconfigured in pursuit of total liberation.

Critical rhetoric is a mode of rhetorical theory and praxis that identifies and critiques ideologies embedded in rhetorical texts. Ideology is "a political language, preserved in rhetorical documents, with the capacity to dictate decision and control public belief and behavior" (McGee, 1980, pp. 3–4). It is ultimately a rhetorical creation constituted and reconstituted through discourse. Critical rhetoricians thus rhetorically contextualize discursive artifacts. They might assess not only what is *in* a text but also what is *absent* from a text, for when dealing with historical and contemporary conflicts, stakeholders often disregard alternative choices that should have been considered (Wander, 2011). Rhetorical contextualization must consider the author (who they are/are not), the audience (who is addressed/who is not), the exigence to which the rhetoric responds (what is it/what is it not), and the solutions articulated (what are they/what are they not). Like critical animal studies, critical rhetorical studies is both descriptive and prescriptive. In other words, critics both assess what is persuasively effective or ineffective about a text and critique its undergirding ontological and/or moral principles to help create a better world.

Critical rhetoric seeks to "counter the excesses of a society's own enabling actions. . .that underwrites the continuation of social practices that ultimately are harmful to the community" (McKerrow, 1989, p. 108). To do so, rhetorical critics explore the reciprocal relationships between domination and freedom. A dialectical approach to these categories invites debate and discussion over two opposing forces while not casting them as always and already separate. Domination—the forced exertion of state or institutional power onto oppressed publics—can occur in tandem with Freedom—the pursuit or experience of equal power relationships among publics. Therefore, critical rhetoricians engage in two simultaneous tasks: "critiques of domination" and "critiques of freedom." Critiquing domination refers to the identification and dismantling of state and institutional power in particular rhetorical texts. Critiquing freedom, however, is much more pertinent to *praxis*-oriented scholarship insomuch as it identifies how *even freedom-fighters* can recreate domineering systems through the promulgation of oppressive logics. In other words, whether "cast as a critique of domination or of freedom, the **initial task** of a critical rhetoric is one of **re-creation**—constructing an argument that identifies the integration of power and knowledge and delineates the role of power/knowledge in structuring social practices" (McKerrow, 1989, p. 102).

In the following sections, I simultaneously critique domination (the systemic and violent realities of speciesism and ableism in everyday life) and freedom (the use of ableism to fight speciesism). In so doing, I offer up an alternative rhetoric of freedom as a prescriptive remedy wherein disability and animal liberation activists are identified as mutual stakeholders in the fight for total liberation.

Eco-Ableism as Rhetorical Form

PETA's "Got Autism?" campaign is rhetorically unsound first and foremost because it employs a rhetoric of "eco-ableism" (Wolbring, 2012). Ableism refers to the unequal power relationships between bodies designated as "abled" and those as "disabled." It often occurs through a "medical model" of disability in which bodies are labeled substandard and abnormal by scientific authorities. An alternate model is the "social model" of disability that understands disabilities not as inherently bad or wrong or in need of resolution, but rather a product of social norms and standards. Thus, while a person might have a different physical and/or mental body compared to the "average" citizen, it is *society* that disables them more so than the body itself.

Eco-ableism, meanwhile, sits at the intersection of speciesism and ableism. The term is often applied in situations wherein environmental activists push for individual behavioral changes or systemic policy changes that would disproportionately harm disabled people. It can also be applied to state and corporate institutions that, through their inaction on existential threats like climate change, put disabled people at extreme risk of poverty, injury, or early death. The term, however, is largely based in a speciesist ontology. The social capital that comes with the abled body is premised upon the elevation of the human over the nonhuman (Taylor, 2017). The able-bodied human subject is considered the peak form of humanness and thus a preferred model of the *homo sapien* species. Disabled bodies are thus rendered to slightly-human, subhuman, or nonhuman status. Their dehumanization (and corresponding animalization) are ideologically related to speciesism insomuch as the disabled body is rendered a species abnormality—something that, if natural selection could only work a little faster, would eliminate them from the human gene pool.

To properly critique PETA's discursive tactics, it is important to understand ableism and eco-ableism as *rhetorical forms*. That is to say, ableism relies upon argumentative schematics that, once identified, are simple to dismantle. Cherney (2011) asserted that "rhetoric can shape the way disability is understood and (in)forms its political implications" (para. 1). After all, "ableist culture sustains and perpetuates itself via rhetoric" (para. 2). Without keen insight into the rhetorical construction of ability and disability, it is all too easy for ableism to prosper, for "ableism is that most insidious form of rhetoric that has become reified and so widely accepted as common sense that it denies its own rhetoricity—it 'goes without saying'" (Cherney, 2011, para. 2). To pursue total liberation, "identifying ableism as rhetoric and exploring its systems dynamic" offers opportunities to identify and/or suggest "corrective practices to refine the successful techniques, reinvent those that fail, and realize new tactics" (Cherney, 2011, para. 2).

By and large, autism and its related co-morbidities are considered disabilities. Under a medical model of disability, autism is a disability insomuch as it is a neurotype that is unusual compared to the general population, thus resulting in behaviors often considered undesirable and in need of medical resolution through actions such as behavioral modification or the development of prenatal autism testing. Under a social model, allistic (nonautistic) neurotypes are understood as having more social capital than autistic neurotypes, thus resulting in a society that inevitably disciplines and disables autistic bodies. The only "cure" for autism is the dissolution of ableism, since without ableism, autism would not be devalued or feared. In PETA's "Got Autism" campaign, it is easy to see how, as Cherney explained, "ableism becomes most visible as a 'mental framework' transmitted through rhetorical devices including language, imagery, and systems of representation" (Cherney, 2011, para. 3).

Within rhetorical studies, it is largely understood that rhetorical moments occur in response to an outside exigence. However, that exigence is molded and shaped through the agenda and spin of the rhetors themselves. In this case, PETA employs a combination of visual and textual artifacts in response to a rhetorical exigence: the existence and mediated scrutiny of autistic bodies. That autistic people exist is not up for debate. However, to promote veganism, PETA makes salient the possible connection of animal consumption and autistic neurotypes.

To understand the building blocks of PETA's argument, I examine their use of argumentative *stases* (the building-blocks of rhetorical problems). The stases are, essentially, rhetorical equations that need only the addition of situation-specific variables to form a coherent argument. The study of rhetorical stases dates all the way back to ancient Greece and Rome (Dieter, 1950). Contemporary studies of stases most typically emphasize five: stases of fact, definition, cause-effect, evaluation, and proposal (Fahnestock & Secor, 1988). In the case of PETA, I focus on three of these stases. First and foremost, they employ the stasis of cause and effect, where the typical model is x occurs due to y. In this case, autism (or in the later version, autistic behavior) is said to occur via dairy consumption. To prove this link, they offer (outdated and disproven) studies suggesting a causal connection between diet and autism. Having offered "evidence" of the link between dairy and autism, PETA employs the stasis of evaluation. Evaluational arguments employ moral reasoning and take the form of: x is good/bad. Given the sad face in the cereal bowl and the explanation of autism as undesirable, PETA hopes that the audience will accept autism as bad. Finally, hoping that the audience accepts this causal link and moral evaluation, PETA then employs a proposal stasis, wherein because of x, a person should do y. Expectedly, PETA's solution to dairy-caused autism/autistic behavior is to go vegan.

In the following sections, I critique PETA's eco-ableist argumentative premises. I do so by deconstructing their manufactured scientific controversy. I ultimately conclude that they offer insufficient backing for their cause and effect argument as well as an eco-ableist rational for their evaluational argument. I then offer a revision of both their evaluational *and* proposal arguments in a manner that maintains PETA's push toward a universal vegan ethic while disavowing the eco-ableist arguments that it used to get there. In so doing, I offer a rationale for viewing autisticness and animality as inherently intertwined ideological concepts with emancipatory possibilities.

Rhetorical Criticism: Manufactured Scientific Controversy

PETA's "Got Autism" campaign is eco-ableist in its rationale and counterproductive to an ethic of total liberation. To fully understand why, it is necessary to probe into how it (mis)uses the rhetoric of science to further its campaign. The rhetorical construction of a scientific "fact" relies upon the "consensus" of the scientific community. A proper scientist understands science as a series of communal expert agreements always open to new data and discoveries. A scientific fact is a fact insomuch as communal expert consensus has rhetorically constructed it as such. That is not to say that "nothing" is ever "true," only that the notion of scientific discourse as separate from rhetoric and persuasion is false. In this section, I explain how PETA exploits the contingent nature of scientific consensus about autism to create a "manufactured scientific controversy." In doing so, it relies upon public misunderstanding of scientific rhetoric to construct its eco-ableist argument for animal rights.

According to Ceccarelli (2011), a scientific controversy is "manufactured" when "an arguer announces that there is an ongoing scientific debate in the technical sphere about a matter for which there is actually an overwhelming scientific consensus" (p. 196). Arguers typically hold significant political, social, or economic capital and are thus able to disseminate their messages far and wide. A prototypical example is political debates over the existence of climate change because, for instance, "the science isn't all in." Perhaps more relevant to this chapter are homeopathic medicinal industries' argumentative linkage of vaccination to autism, wherein stakeholders blame "Big Pharma" for duping innocent publics into injecting their children with neurodiversity. Fundamental to this genre of rhetoric is *disingenuousness*. Whereas an audience may genuinely believe the scientific nonfacts they are being told (climate change is fake; vaccines cause autism), the rhetors themselves are predominantly looking to further bolster their political, social, and/or economic capital. They *may* believe what they are saying, but they very well may not. What matters most is getting an audience to adhere to their argument by any means necessary, even through the purposeful distortion of the scientific process. In other words, a manufactured scientific controversy functions as "a special type of 'public scientific controversy' in which 'strategically distorted communication' works to corrode the democratic process" (Ceccarelli, 2011, p. 196).

Manufactured scientific controversy functions through a series of discursive strategies. First, rhetors initiate *either* an "epistemological filibuster" (Ceccarelli, 2011, p. 197) as a means to delay sociopolitical change (climate change is fake, so don't regulate carbon emissions) *or* a "fairplay wedge" (p. 197) to enact sociopolitical change (vaccines cause autism), so teach the controversy and don't mandate vaccination. Second, rhetors exploit "conventional ignorance" of the scientific process by picking and choosing scientific papers in which articles "are taken out of context, data is cherry-picked, and statistical methods are manipulated with evaluation standards being strengthened for studies that have inconvenient results" (p. 197). Finally, rhetors make their faulty claims difficult to counter through the deployment of "discursive traps" (p. 202), specifically, the exploitations of "balancing norms" in journalism and the topoi of "freedom of speech and freedom of inquiry" (p. 218). Past studies of manufactured scientific controversies thus "tell the story of a powerful argumentative tactic that is difficult to counter" (p. 202).

Despite the rhetorical power of manufactured scientific controversy, there are a series of rhetorical tactics to counter such arguments. These tactics rely upon the study of rhetorical stases. When confronted with a manufactured scientific controversy, counter-arguers should "engage the opponents claims but then explicitly shift the stasis from questions of fact, definition and cause to the questions of value and policy that are the driving force behind the public debate" (Ceccarelli, 2011, p. 211). Further, critics should "point to the 'smoking gun' memos and other indicators that scientific controversy is being manufactured to manipulate a public audience in these cases" while "taking care not to adopt a dismissive tone toward everyone who takes a skeptical view toward mainstream science" (Ceccarelli, 2011, p. 211). Upon completing these tasks, audiences should (at least in theory) be able to understand that they have been duped by disingenuous rhetors. In other words, through the identification and deconstruction of a manufactured scientific controversy, critical animal studies scholars and activists can engage in prescriptive scholarship that promotes the *responsible* invocation of scientific inquiry, consensus, and doubt in the pursuit of total liberation.

In keeping with Ceccarelli's recommendation, I will first engage with PETA's stasis of cause and effect. Inserting a "fairplay wedge" into a nondebate over dairy and autism, PETA suggests the *possibility* of causal connection between the two and that the science is not all in. They consistently hedge their claims with phrases like "More research is needed" and "the reason why dairy 'products' may worsen autism is *being debated*" (PETA, n.d., para. 1–2, emphasis mine) But, "*Regardless of the cause,* testimonials show that many people with this condition may be able to find relief with a simple dietary change" (para. 3, emphasis mine).

Using these hedging statements affords PETA plausible deniability by acknowledging the indeterminacy of their claims. However, as a manufactured scientific controversy always does, PETA's emphasis on further research and debate suggests an ongoing scientific argument where there is none. Scientific consensus denies a link between diet and autism. Further, the sources they offer are both outdated. Both studies came from the University of Rome in 1995 and the other in 2002 (Knivsberg et al., 2002; Lucarelli et al., 1995). The studies are not comprehensive enough to suggest a causal link between diet and autism, meaning that PETA is misrepresenting the conclusions. Both utilized extremely small sample sizes of people (20 and 36, respectively) and neither concluded a direct causal link between dairy and autistic behavior (the first tested casein- and gluten-free dietary interventions for children with urinary peptide abnormalities) and (the second linked food allergies with infantile autism). Furthermore, disciplinary reviews have rendered both PETA's studies obsolete (Mari-Bauset et al., 2014; Mulloy et al., 2010). PETA's stasis of cause-and-effect is therefore toothless. Its only power relies upon the scientific illiteracy of its audience.

However, through the creation of a manufactured scientific controversy, PETA's "Got Autism" campaign functioned as a rhetorical "image event"—a staged act of protest designed for mass media dissemination (Delicath & DeLuca, 2003). Under a dissemination model of communication, the specific content of a message is less important than how widespread the message becomes. Efficacy is measured by a text's virality. Because of its mass-mediated coverage, PETA was able to utilize the news media genre's ethic of "balanced" coverage to further its fairplay wedge. Journalistic texts are expected to show more than one "side" of a single story. However, this generic trope often leads audience to the impression that an issue is more controversial than it actually is, or that one "side" of the story is more scientifically credible than it is. Coverage of PETA offered in-depth explanations of the defunct theories inherent in its premises, including the disproven "leaky gut theory" of autism and the "opoid effect" (Kluger, 2014; Salahi, 2008).

PETA's untrue cause-effect stasis only bolstered its evaluative and proposal stases. After all, determining a "cause" is only important if society cares about the existence of the "effect." The "Got Autism?" campaign functioned by evaluating autism in children as something morally bad and in need of fixing. In other words, it proposed a dairy-free diet to fix the inherent badness of autistic children—a rhetoric of eco-ableism. PETA has evaluatively linked autism to life-threatening and painful medical conditions in need of aggressive treatment: "It isn't surprising that dairy products may worsen this condition, considering that milk has already been strongly linked to cancer, Crohn's disease, and other serious health problems" (PETA, n.d., para. 6). In response to PETA's campaign, ill-informed parents of autistic children and high-ranking members of exploitative autism nonprofits were given platforms through which they could evaluate autism as a tragedy in need of fixing through even controversial methods such as a vegan diet. This voice included Shelley Reynolds, president of the controversial group, Unlocking Autism. Reynolds claimed, "There are not a lot of things you can control in autism, but you can control your child's diet...We don't hold parallel views with PETA, but I think that anything that sheds light on the autism crisis is awesome" (qtd. in Salahi, 2008, para. 16). Michelle Guppy of Texas Autism Advocacy furthered PETA's narrative: "If [the billboard] alerts parents to potential issues that are valid, then I don't much care who is putting it on" (paras. 17–18). And Gillian Loughran, editor of *Autism Eye*, concluded PETA's fairplay wedge by writing that "numerous parents are making the switch" to a casein-free diet, so PETA "left it up to individual families to decide what to do...knowledge is power. And I don't see a problem with that" (qtd. in PETA, 2014, paras. 6, 10).

Ultimately, however, PETA's eco-ableist campaign functioned as a manufactured controversy because of the organization's disingenuousness. There is a "smoking gun" that demonstrates PETA's ulterior motive: They did not genuinely believe that dairy causes autism but wanted to sow the seeds of doubt in order to promote their vegan agenda. By demonizing autism and attributing its moral wrongness to dairy, PETA strategically constructed a nonexigence to get attention for animal rights. However, they did so by secretly editing their campaign's main argument in the hopes that no one would notice their discursive shifts over time. A rhetorical analysis of PETA's shift from hyperbolic fear-mongering to hedged and passive claims demonstrates how the organization artfully changed its theses to further its own cause, suggesting that the organization does not necessarily believe its own claims insomuch as it wishes to simply convert audiences to veganism.

Contemporarily, PETA's rhetors strategically shift the blame to scientific and activist outlets for paying attention to the (undated) webpage. When the campaign gained attention in 2014, PETA spokespeople said that the campaign was no longer running and merely "revived by the media" (Anders, 2014, para. 7). However, an assessment of the website's edits over time proves this is not the case. In 2017 a PETA spokesman reiterated to *The Mighty*: "This is an old campaign that is still on our website because we have heard from people who have said it contains helpful information" (qtd. in Davidson, 2017, para. 6). In other words, PETA rhetorically distanced itself from responsibility for its thesis while at the same time leaving its (undated) website available for audience consumption.

However, this has most definitely *not* ended its "Got Autism?" campaign. Instead, over time, it has silently and secretly edited the content of its message to suit mainstream discourses about autism, moving from a "causal crisis" narrative to a "correlative concern" narrative. PETA has not admitted to this fact, but internet archives such as the "Way Back Machine" tell the tale. From 2008 to 2013, PETA's "Got Autism?" campaign utilized a causal crisis narrative that depicted autism as a dangerous disease directly caused by dairy consumption. Its language was dramatic and based in fear appeals. Their website categorized autism as a "brain disorder" and a "devastating disease" marked by "anti-social behavior" that "takes an enormous toll on sufferers and their families" (PETA, 2013, para. 1). The initial thesis stated that "dairy foods may worsen or even cause autism" and thus "anyone who wants to alleviate or avoid the devastating effects of autism should give cow's milk the boot" (paras. 3, 6).

However, the digital content originally said that the site now takes a more measured tone. Internet archives show that the linguistic shifts began in 2013 and have continued slowly and minutely to this day. In keeping with mainstream discursive shifts about autism being a "disease" to a "condition," PETA now claims that "autism and autism spectrum disorder are complex disorders of brain development" (PETA, n.d., para. 1). Words such as "devastating" have been removed, as have references to the destruction of the family unit. Most importantly, however, PETA has deleted *direct* causal claims about dairy consumption and autism, instead pointing to autistic *behaviors* and suggesting that a casein-free diet might *lessen* them.

This shift in discourse is a "smoking gun" for two reasons: First, it shows how PETA has disingenuously called its own campaign "old" and "defunct." Although it has distanced itself from its own problematic claims about autism, it has not only left the 2008 website running but has also continued editing the website's content to this day. But perhaps more important is the second reason: PETA has dramatically shifted its original causal argument over time while still relying upon the same set of defunct studies. This suggests that PETA has not changed its stance because it has received new information (which would be a rhetorically responsible thing to do) but has rather edited its own claims *without* new information. I posit that PETA is aware that its original cited studies did not causally prove a connection between dairy and autism. I further suggest that PETA has adjusted its tone not due to new information about neurodiversity but because it wanted to make the not-defunct campaign more palatable to parents wanting to "fix" undesirable autistic behaviors.

PETA's manufactured scientific controversy thus functions by denying the campaign's existence even though it still exists, simultaneously claiming and not claiming a causal link between dairy and autism, and utilizing ableist tropes that, whether hyperbolic or not, depict autistic behaviors as inherently bad. Its arguments rely upon an unscientific causal stasis, an ableist evalua-tive stasis, and a proposal stasis that makes little sense due to the factual and ethical insufficiencies of the prior two stases. It is therefore an eco-ableist argument that does little for the pursuit of total liberation.

Rhetorical Reformation: Dismantling Ableist-Speciesist Nexus

As I mentioned previously, critical rhetoric is attuned to the goals of critical animal studies in that it not only describes problematic behavior on the part of rhetors but also prescribes possible solutions to those problems consis-tent with the ethical standpoint of the critic. As an autistic vegan scholar, I will use this section not to further "trash" PETA, but rather to offer animal liberationists an opportunity to use the lessons learned from the harmful "Got Autism?" to construct more effective and ethical arguments for the total liberation of species. More specifically, I will identify how autism and animality have been inextricably linked through discourse and how, through the careful consideration of both ableism *and* speciesism, animal and autistic liberation can be pursued at once. Dismantling the ableist-speciesist nexus is integral to the pursuit of total liberation.

PETA's "Got Autism" campaign relied upon the linkage of autism and undesirable behavior. Had they considered the interconnections of ableism and speciesism, they might have found how autistic people have been advocating for a redefinition of their "undesirable behaviors"—and thus, a reiteration of their personhood. In particular, autistic activists deplore prototypical therapies for autistic children including applied behavioral analysis (ABA). Activists have been known to call the therapy "dog training for children." Argumentatively linking Pavlov's historically cruel experiments on canines to the forceful annihilation of autistic children's natural behaviors, they ask for allistic people to treat autistic children with dignity and respect instead of demanding assimilation through aversive training mechanisms. Here as well is a possible interconnection of autistic and animal advocacy. As an autistic person, I understand that my behaviors do not often correspond to what is considered natural and normal in human society. For adherents ABA practitioners, to become "normal" and thus fully and properly human requires me to disavow my normal instincts and endure psychological harm for the comfort of allistic people.

As an animal liberationist, I further identify the disavowal of ABA as "dog training," as a tacit agreement among stakeholders that there is something morally wrong with forcing an animal to do as a human pleases using violent and aversive techniques. I see myself in the dog with the prong collar having its nose rubbed in feces. I see myself in the orca at SeaWorld jumping through hoops for the amusement of others. I jump through metaphorical hoops every day to function in an ableist world and feel my invisible prong collar tugging at my flesh whenever my mask slips. In advocating for neurodiversity, I simultaneously advocate for animal liberation. My version of liberation is not based in segregation of species, but rather as the peaceful coexistence of interconnected moral subjects. Autistic people do not need to live on a different planet from allistics to thrive; animals do not need to live on a separate continent from humans to live in peace. However, both parties must be *embraced* for their differences, for their alterity, and for their "significant otherness" (Haraway, 2003). My companion species' instinct to chew on a carpet when anxious does not justify me crating her until I come home from work, where her paws are drenched in sweat from being cooped up in a tiny space all day. My instinct to stim by twirling my fingers or repeating phrases under my breath does not justify sending me to therapy for forty hours a week until my parents feel satisfied that they can raise me without stress. There are different ways to coexist; there are different means of coming to mutual understanding and acceptance. Dismantling the ableist-speciesist nexus is one way to find them.

Animals are consistently denied their subjectivity, personhood, and rights on the basis that they are not morally capable of appreciating them. Measures of relational morality are typically measured through human standards of self-consciousness. Specifically, they are assessed through neuro-ableist categorizations of emotionality and relationality. These concepts, often measured through measures of *empathy*, has been used to deny animals and humans of their agency and subsequently their rights. Rene Descartes in particular is famous for his definition of animals as "mere automata" whose cries of pain were equivalent to a squeaking cog in a machine. Cognitive ethologists, such as Mark Bekoff, have been trying to demonstrate the incoherency of such statements by showing the rich emotional and moral lives of animal subjects. Even though animals might not express emotions or inhabit relationships that are *the same* as humans, they are nonetheless fully capable of feeling and relating. Their sentience, therefore, is grounds for the appreciation of their rights and personhood.

I also identify with the metaphor of an amoral, unfeeling automaton. I remember my high school theatre teacher calling me a "robot" whose emotions were either missing or unconvincing. Autistic activists seek to dismantle the rhetorical constructions of their inherent amorality and unemotionality. Autistic individuals are often typecast as self-absorbed, unemotional people incapable of empathy. This is largely a result of psychiatric hypotheses that autistic people lack "Theory of Mind"—the ability to grasp what another person might be thinking or feeling at a given moment (Baron-Cohen, 1997). As a result, it is assumed that we are incapable of emotionally connecting with other people. Autistic activists and psychological researchers are trying to dismantle this hypothesis through counter-theories such as "Intense World Syndrome," which suggests that autistic people actually feel *more* than allistic individuals and thus present emotions differently (Markram & Markram, 2010). They also note the differentiation between cognitive empathy and affective empathy, wherein autistic people may struggle with the former but are good at the latter (Rogers et al., 2007). Regardless, a subject's ability to "feel" or "emote" according to neurotypical standards should not be a basis for denying one's rights. Furthermore, compassion and empathy are hardly the same thing—I may at times present as a robot, but I am fully capable of believing in and fighting for an ethic of total liberation.

Finally, animals and autistic people are consistently categorized according to ableist standards of cognition. That is to say, we are typecast as persons or nonpersons by virtue of our ability to measure up to standards of intellect and rationality. One way in which this occurs is through the definition of language. Many rhetoricians identify argumentation and persuasion as the exclusive domain of humans. We are, after all, the only beings with phoneme- and morpheme-centered language and written texts that cohere to that spoken language. The ability to verbally "speak" is identified as a marker of cognitive capacity. Because many autistic individuals are fully or partially nonverbal, they become symbolically "voiceless" and thus considered incapable of advocating for themselves. Their voicelessness is further compounded by "functioning labels" wherein autistic subjects deemed "low functioning" are considered too cognitively deficient to advocate for their interests in any coherent way and "high-functioning" autistic people are typecast as too neurotypical to understand what a low-functioning autistic person needs. This enables exploitative organizations such as Autism Speaks to construct themselves as the "Voice of the Voiceless" and speak *for* autistic people instead of *with* them. Autistic activists are therefore pushing for the deconstruction of spoken language as a measure of intellect and the dissolution of functioning labels as a measure of personhood.

Because of these struggles, I identify with the plight of animals deemed too brutish or stupid to deserve rights. Casting humans as the top of the moral food change due to their particular cognitive capacities is a speciesist-ableist endeavor. Just because a deer does not cry "no!" when confronted with a hunter's gun does not mean it has no interest in living. Just because a gerbil is not as adept at using tools as a chimpanzee does not mean that the former deserves fewer rights than the latter. At the same time, I am upset at the rhetorical tactics of animal rights activists who play into ableist depictions of language and intellect to argue for (exceedingly limited) animal rights and personhood. I am disdained at how legal arguments for animal personhood are based in particular species' particularly "advanced" cognitive skills. I am equally disgusted with animal rights organizations such as "Anonymous for the Voiceless" that in their very name disavow the potential of animal communication. Animals are perfectly capable of advocating for themselves if only humans would listen more closely.

In closing, PETA's "Got Autism?" campaign was offensive as offensive could be. They were factually wrong to link autism to dairy consumption. However, they were not wrong to argumentatively link autism and animality. Because ableism and speciesism intersect, because the construction of the ideal human subject is based in depictions of an able-bodied and cognitively advanced neurotypical person, both autistic people and animals are oppressed for their differences. Because both critical rhetoric and critical animal studies are descriptive *and* prescriptive, I have offered a series of revisions to PETA's faulty logic that compassionately link the struggles of autistic people and animals. Disability and animal liberation are intertwined, so either struggle should be exploited for the advancement of the other.

Concluding Remarks

This chapter critiqued the "Got Autism?" campaign put forth by PETA. From 2008 to the present day, PETA has utilized visual and digital media to attribute autism and its physical comorbidities to the consumption of dairy. As an autistic individual, a total liberationist vegan, and a critical rhetorician, I used my lived experience and rhetorical expertise to perform a "critique of freedom" in response to PETA's anti-dairy ad campaign. I ultimately argued that PETA's campaign was and is counterproductive to an ethic of total liberation due to its eco-ableist framework, its unethical production of manufactured scientific controversy, and its missed opportunity to address the interconnected and often analogous oppressions faced by nonhuman animals and autistic individuals.

I hope that this chapter will not be interpreted as mere "PETA bashing" or "scholarly neval-gazing." On the contrary, my goal is that scholars, advocates, and activists committed to total liberation will see the value in critical rhetoric not only as an academic theory but also as an activist praxis. Rhetorical criticism is a useful means through which to address the strategies and tactics of animal rights activists and their campaigns. In deconstructing the argumentative frameworks undergirding campaigns such as PETA's, freedom fighters committed to human and nonhuman animal justice can more easily identify which master-discourses are productive or counterproductive to a goal of total liberation. Words matter, and when those words are ordered into coherent arguments, the words matter even more. When assessing if a rhetor has successfully utilized the available means of persuasion to achieve their ends, a critical standpoint toward both domination and freedom is essential to productive exchanges between different social justice stakeholders. As Ari Ne'eman stated in his critique of PETA's "Got Autism" campaign, "by challenging the exploitative and offensive public discourse on disability we find today, we can advance a broader agenda for disability rights" (Ne'eman, 2008b, para. 9). I supplement this statement: By challenging exploitative and offensive public discourse on disability *and* speciesism, we advance a broader agenda for *total liberation*.

References

Anders, C. J. (2014, May 28). "PETA tries to pretend dairy products have something to do with autism." *Gizmodo*. https://io9.gizmodo.com/peta-tries-to-pretend-dairy-products-have-something-to-1582896128

Baron-Cohen, S. (1997). *Mindblindness: An essay on autism and theory of mind*. MIT press.

Best, S. (2009). The rise of critical animal studies: Putting theory into action and animal liberation into higher education. *Journal for Critical Animal Studies*, *7*(1), 9–52.

Best, S. (2014). *The politics of total liberation: Revolution for the 21st century*. Springer.

Ceccarelli, L. (2011). Manufactured scientific controversy: Science, rhetoric, and public debate. *Rhetoric & Public Affairs*, *14*(2), 195–228.

Cherney, J. L. (2011). The rhetoric of ableism. *Disability Studies Quarterly*, *31*(3). Retrieved from http://dsq-sds.org/article/view/1665/1606

Davidson, J. (2017, September 8). "Old PETA campaign linking milk to autism has people outraged." *The Mighty*. Retrieved from https://themighty.com/2017/09/peta-got-autism-campaign/

Delicath, J. W., & DeLuca, K. M. (2003). Image events, the public sphere, and argumentative practice: The case of radical environmental groups. *Argumentation*, *17*(3), 315–333.

Dieter, O. A. L. (1950). Stasis. *Communications Monographs*, *17*(4), 345–369.

Fahnestock, J., & Secor, M. (1988). The stases in scientific and literary argument. *Written Communication*, *5*(4), 427–443.

Haraway, D. J. (2003). *The companion species manifesto: Dogs, people, and significant otherness*. Chicago: Prickly Paradigm Press.

Kluger, J. (2014, May 30). "Got credibility? Then you're not PETA." *Time*. Retrieved from https://time.com/2798480/peta-autism-got-milk/.

Knivsberg, A. M., Reichelt, K. L., Høien, T., & Nødland, M. (2002). A randomised, controlled study of dietary intervention in autistic syndromes. *Nutritional Neuroscience*, *5*(4), 251–261.

Lucarelli, S., Frediani, T., Zingoni, A. M., Ferruzzi, F., Giardini, O., Quintieri, F., Barbato, M., D'eufemia, E., & Cardi, E. (1995). Food allergy and infantile autism. *Panminerva Medica*, *37*(3), 137–141.

Mari-Bauset, S., Zazpe, I., Mari-Sanchis, A., Llopis-González, A., & Morales-Suarez-Varela, M. (2014). Evidence of the gluten-free and casein-free diet in autism spectrum disorders: A systematic review. *Journal of Child Neurology*, *29*(12), 1718–1727.

Markram, K., & Markram, H. (2010). The intense world theory–a unifying theory of the neurobiology of autism. *Frontiers in Human Neuroscience*, *4*, 224.

Matusitz, J., & Forrester, M. (2013). PETA making social noise: A perspective on shock advertising. *Portuguese Journal of Social Science*, *12*(1), 85–100.

McGee, M. C. (1980). The "ideograph": A link between rhetoric and ideology. *Quarterly Journal of Speech*, *66*(1), 1–16.

McKerrow, R. E. (1989). Critical rhetoric: Theory and praxis. *Communications Monographs*, *56*(2), 91–111.

Mulloy, A., Lang, R., O'Reilly, M., Sigafoos, J., Lancioni, G., & Rispoli, M. (2010). Gluten-free and casein-free diets in the treatment of autism spectrum disorders: A systematic review. *Research in Autism Spectrum Disorders*, *4*(3), 328–339.

Ne'Eman, A. (2008, October 21). "PETA billboard removed." Autism Self Advocacy Network [blog post]. Retrieved from https://autisticadvocacy.org/2008/10/peta-billboard-removed/

Ne'eman, A. (2008a). "Tell PETA to stop exploiting the autistic community." *iPetitions*. Retrieved from https://www.ipetitions.com/petition/autismPETA

PETA. (2013) "Got autism? Learn about the link between dairy products and the disease." Retrieved from https://web.archive.org/web/20131205141644/ https://www.peta.org/features/got-autism-learn-link-dairy-products-disease/

PETA. (2014, June 6). "My son has autism—that's why I support PETA's autism campaign." Retrieved from https://www.peta.org/blog/dairy-autism-letter/

PETA (n.d.). "Learn about the link between dairy and autism." Retrieved from https://www.peta.org/features/got-autism-learn-link-dairy-products-disease/

Rogers, K., Dziobek, I., Hassenstab, J., Wolf, O. T., & Convit, A. (2007). Who cares? Revisiting empathy in Asperger syndrome. *Journal of Autism and Developmental Disorders, 37*(4), 709–715.

Salahi, L. (2008, September 17). "PETA campaign angers autism groups." *ABC News*. Retrieved from https://abcnews.go.com/Health/MindMoodNews/story?id=5923337&page=1&singlePa=true

Taylor, S. (2017). *Beasts of burden: Animal and disability liberation*. The New Press.

Wander, P. C. (2011). On ideology: Second thoughts. *Western Journal of Communication, 75*(4), 421–428.

Wolbring, G. (2012). Eco-ableism. *Anthropology News, 14*. Retrieved from https://www.anthropology-news.org/2012/09/14/eco-ableism/.

2. Getting to Solidarity: Toward an Interest-Based Conflict Resolution Approach to Resolving the Conflict between Ecoability Equity and Animal Equity

DANIEL SALOMON

Introduction

As someone who is neurodiverse, I need diverse communities to fully acknowledge ability as one expression of diversity. In addition, I need mutual respect and accountability; fairness, consistency, and transparency of social norms (instead of a double standard); and civility and nonviolent communication. Most importantly, I need to have the opportunity to learn from where each person is coming from.

Ableism affects me through two narratives of autism: tragedy and supercrip. A supercrip is a sample token individual in one of the ability communities who is seen by white society as able to assimilate into white society and is singled out for the purpose of promotion, in the process, making nondisabled peoples feel good about themselves and shaming the rest of us. The tragedy narrative that I have received for most of my forty years incorrectly portrays autistic people as useless. The tragedy narrative has led to exclusion from professional level employment that is appropriate to my level of education and skill. While society has for the most part gotten beyond the tragedy narrative, it is still stuck on the supercrip narrative of autism. I have personally run into as part of my lived experiences some who say superstars on the autism spectrum like Temple Grandin is "the new normal," which *everyone* with autism must live up to, to become leaders and have representation (See Grandin *Talent's*, 2020) for what she expects from others on the autism spectrum and Bernick and Holden as an example of transforming Grandin's expectations into new social norms for "high-functioning" autistic peoples). Grandin is a consultant to the livestock industry on animal behavior and an autism spokesperson (Grandin). All I want to do in the second half of my life is to work, do what I am good at, and make a difference for our planet in peril.

This chapter will respectfully, sympathetically, and generously engage the various animal movements to rethink the relationship between ecoability equity and animal equity, from the perspectives of ethics, critical theory, political advocacy, conflict resolution, and urban studies. I will include a critique of Grandin, the relationships possible between neurodiverse humans and animals and a social justice alternative to the typical purist or behaviorist approaches to the relationship between neurodiverse humans and animals in critical animal studies circles and critical disability studies circles.

I will also work with my lived experiences with animals, and involvement with the animal movements as a model, to show the types of compassionate relationships possible between neurodiverse humans and animals, as well as the potentially constructive role that peoples of all abilities could play in the furthering of the animal movements.

A Critique of Temple Grandin

Grandin has accomplished some of the goals of animal welfare through using her autistic mammalian mind to empathize with the emotional needs of animals, combined with sound animal behavior science and taking a pragmatic, reformist approach (Grandin). Grandin not only invented an operational "humane" slaughter system using the above criteria but also persuaded one half of slaughterhouses in the United States to use her system. She even has developed animal welfare audits which McDonald's uses and reveres (Grandin).

There is a radical animal liberation complaint against Grandin. Mainly, she's too animal welfare (cruelty like factory farming can continue as long as it is done humanely) versus animal abolition (cruelty needs to be eliminated because animal rights are inalienable rights). As an animal liberation advocate myself, my sympathies lie with abolition, not welfare.

As a neurodiverse scholar with a strong liberal arts background, I have concerns about Grandin's social conservatism and sociological naiveté which she seems to apply consistently to both animals and neurodiverse humanity alike. She takes an apolitical "blame the victim," "life is not fair," "these are the way things are" approach to animals, neurodiverse humans, and even herself. Seeing society as this natural entity, which from a sociological perspective is anything but "natural" (Grandin).

Grandin uses machine metaphors to describe animals and humans alike, even making comments like "this animal was ruined!" "This autistic was ruined!" (Grandin) when describing our mistakes and misfortunes, implying that our lives are "replaceable parts in a complicated machine" (Grandin).

The most disturbing flaw is not Grandin's or the animal movements' fault. The neurodiversity community has been hit particularly hard by the same assimilationist-tokenism which has impacted the disability community at-large. Grandin has been "the token" for the autistic community, allowed to speak uninterrupted, as white society's appointed ambassador of the autistic community, on all matters of autistic self-understanding including animals (e.g., Bernick and Holden).

This is before the community at-large has had a chance to speak. As a result, the animal movements have gotten the impression that every person on the autism spectrum has views about animals just like Grandin. In reality, if the entire community had the opportunity to speak on behalf of animal kind, normative animal groups would learn that some members go farther than Grandin's welfare. For example, esteemed autistic pride activist Jim Sinclair ( ) is a vegan (Sinclair). Grandin is not the only autistic animal show in town.

This is not to mention that Grandin's branding of high-functioning autism is a very specific racial, ethnic, cultural, nationalistic, generational, gender, and geopolitical media portrayal of high-functioning autism. The image of high-functioning autism which Grandin projects is a media image of high-functioning autism which is: white, W.A.S.P. like, Connecticut Yankee like, Boomer, female, and rural American. Not that there is anything wrong with any of these identities but it just does not represent the full plethora of neurodiverse peoples and our subsequent lived experiences.

For example, not all of us who are labeled as high functioning are white, Northern European, Connecticut Yankee-types, from the Boomer generation, female, and from a rural American background. Peoples labeled as high functioning come from all races, ethnicities and nationalities, from all generations, from all genders, and from American cities and suburbs, as well as rural locales around the world.

As Critical Animal Studies scholars, we have the legitimacy to challenge Grandin like you would any other academic, on the grounds of her ideas, like her tacky machine metaphors, her sociological nativity, disagreeing with her animal welfare and the unconscious biases of her media representation and narrative, which promote and perpetuate stereotypes and inequity. As Critical Disability Studies scholars, we need to recover the full spectrum of views about animals in the neurodiversity communities and provide radical alternatives to Grandin and help other neurodiverse voices emerge in academia—in the vanguard, in the media, and in popular culture.

As Critical Disabilities Studies scholars, we need to get beyond mere anecdotal evidence and protest to further disability justice and neurodiversity and start moving in the direction of developing a mixed methodology approach (both qualitative and quantitative) for Critical Disabilities Studies, coupled with "enacting civic engagement and social transformation" (Welch, 2019) so that we could start to develop a positive correlation of ecoability and linked oppressions for the purpose of working toward environmental justice, social equity, and total liberation for peoples of all abilities. This is because "such evidence may be true and verifiable, but it may only represent extraordinary cases" (Diez, Barr & Ketinkaye-Rundel, 2015, p. 22) which is harmful and exclusionary to neurodiversity and absolutely devastating to animals, which is undesirable and unacceptable for neurodiversity as a whole. Instead, "we should examine a sample of many cases that represent the population" (Diez, Barr & Ketinkaye-Rundel, 2015, p. 23), making sure that we collect stories and listen to the silenced voices of peoples on the autism spectrum from all races, nations, tongues, ethnicities, religions, cultures, geopolitical contexts, genders, generations, situations, and political, religious, cultural, economic, and family beliefs about animals.

Ecological Nonviolence: The Autistic-Animal Relationships Possible in the Urban Context

First, I contend that Grandin is right on one thing: because some of us, autistic humans, rely more on our mammalian mind (the member of our mind which evolved from primates which is not unique to today's humans and is different than our reptilian mind which predates our mammalian mind) than neurotypicals (nonautistic humans), we have special insights into the possibility of the existence of animal intelligence (Grandin). The autistic primatologist, Dawn-Prince Hughes (2020), has had a similar experience to Grandin in this regard. Hughes also "personifies inanimate objects," where she used her autistic propensity, to identify the individual personalities of gorillas, subsequently studying gorillas as "non-human persons" (Prince-Huges, *Songs of the Gorilla Nation*). Similarities in my way of being in the world: my mannerisms, ritualized communication, keen senses, and ability to compensate using other members of my brain, I have developed interspecies communications abilities with both domestic and wild animals.

Second, as oppression survivors, surviving being treated as other and inferior, some of us are able to profoundly empathize with the plight of animals who also have been "poorly treated" by white society, recognizing in animal suffering the patterns of our own abuse and oppression.

Grandin who was bullied and isolated growing up was able to recognize fear in animals, identified "reducing fear" and attentiveness to an animal's physical environment as something animals need (Grandin). Prince-Hughes who was also bullied growing up had her conversion to the animal cause when she saw a captive troop of gorillas being teased and taunted at a city zoo. She stood in solidarity with the gorillas the rest of the afternoon and went on to become a primatologist and ape advocate (Prince-Hughes, *Songs of the Gorilla Nation*). Jim Sinclair, who is no stranger to all-around creepy professional relationships, definitely saw a contradiction between Grandin claiming to love animals and calling for their deaths at the same time, where Sinclair publically criticized Grandin's "human slaughter systems," comparing them to modern-day death penalty practices (Sinclair, "An Autistic Activist Responds to Temple Grandin").

Knowing personally what it's like to be targeted and scapegoated for being different, I got my start in animal advocacy, witnessing how wildlife managers were welcoming sports hunters into my suburban home, to target and eradicate overpopulated yet native White Tailed Deer and Canada Geese with guns and crossbows, using propaganda to intimate the animal movements. As a result, I became outspoken against such hunts, testifying at local public meetings. As an undergraduate student, I gave up a promising career in biology, partially because vivisection was against my conscience.

Third, we, the neurodiverse, bring gifts to the animal rights cause. Grandin's gifts to the cause are unrestricted documentation of factory farm practices and malpractices across the country, reducing the most egregiously cruel practices toward animals in big farming through putting "absolute limits" on what these corporations can/cannot do to their own animals, reducing out-and-out scandals, an economic argument for morally considering animals and credible scientific evidence for emotions and intelligence in mammals and birds (Grandin). Prince-Hughes's gifts are standing in solidarity with animal kind, credible scientific evidence for personality and culture in gorillas, coupled with a passion for great ape issues (Prince-Huges, *Songs of the Gorilla Nation*).

Sinclair brings the gifts of an autistic person who is a successful vegan, offering also an autistic critique of Grandin and a devastating critique of the key argument in favor of vivisection (Sinclair, "An Autistic Activist Responds to Temple Grandin").

Animal experimentation ensures safe treatments for incurable conditions (e.g., Kruse, C. R., 2001, "The Movement and the Media: Framing the Debate over Animal Experimentation").

Sinclair implies that in the treatment of autism, vivisection instead projects animal cruelty onto autistic humanity, "treating us as animals," applying Skinner-like Behavioralism on rats and mice, to us, used to violently socialize us into white society (Sinclair, "An Autistic Activist Responds to Temple Grandin").

The gifts I offer are consciously and systematically linking the oppression situations of animals and neurodiverse humanity, situated into a liberal arts and social research context, expanding this discussion to include all members of the animal kingdom and not just mammals (birds, fish, reptiles, amphibians, and invertebrates). I also give these gifts to all life (plants, lichens, funguses, algae, and microorganisms) and the natural elements of air, water, soil, land, fire, light, sound and stars, as well as the planet, the ecological whole, the interconnections, the commons, embodied relations, biogeochemical cycles, and local bioregions Broto & Bulkeley, n.d.). Also, I give these gifts to human eco-justice issues, especially how planetary-level and local environmental disasters impact peoples of all abilities through impacting our health, livability, and connections, as well as ecospirituality issues, especially aesthetics, ecopsychology, deep ecology, men's movements, interspecies communications, and Christian environmentalism.

I also agree that we need many more indigenous, people of color and women of color, autistic ecologies and crip animal ethics (all-access animal ethics), to be recovered and told in first person, as well as more non-Western autistic ecologies and crip animal ethics, from the Geographic South. I even agree that we need to recover, in first person, the autistic ecologies and crip animal ethics of peoples on the autism spectrum who have been labeled low functioning and peoples on the autism spectrum who are nonverbal (deconstruction, empowerment, statistics, and learning from history, see Edith Sheffer, 2018, *Asperger's Children: the Origins of Autism in Nazi Vienna*).

Finally, the urban context offers many unique possibilities for developing nonviolent relationships with animals—individually, collectively, and institutionally—for neurodiverse humans. Interspecies communications with proper physical distance with animals, wild and domesticated, which cannot be hunted and eaten, make it possible for neurodiversity in an urban context, to get to know living animals as sentient beings, not as food, medicine, and clothing.

Neurodiversity, in an urban context, can also access vegan food systems, holistic medicines not experimented on animals, alternatives to furs and leathers, and, most importantly, we have other ways to commune with animals other than sadistic blood sports, bullying entertainment, and needing to slaughter animals to eat and survive.

It is also vitally important as urban autistic ecologists and urban crip animal ethicists that we understand the context, in which we write, advocate, and live in relationship to animals, other humans and the planet as a whole, as our shared home. For example, we need to be sensitive to the long unsavory Western history of hate, structural racism, and political economic inequity which continue to persist as we go deeper into the 21st century (which is my response to Welch). We also need to be sensitive to the histories, cultures and life ways of ingenious peoples around the world, as well as the unique ways many indigenous peoples have traditionally worked with space as place (which is my response to Glendenning). We even need to be sensitive to the reality of class differences between city people and rural people, between professionals and laborers, and between employed and underemployed/unemployed peoples.

Human-Animal Reconciliation: A Crip Urban Animal Ethic

How can animals and neurodiverse humans both get the social justice we deserve through engaging conflict resolution? I am going to offer an alternative which addresses the animal welfare/abolition responses to disability-animal relationships which is not helping anyone anywhere. My alternative also addresses the disability/animal dualism which is a false choice, contending that it's a false choice, when making ethical decisions, to choose between animal rights and disability rights.

Such thinking has its historical and academic origins in Greco-Enlightenment Western ideologies where such Western ideologies are immune to empirical truths. The Western pre-truth ideological logic behind choosing to save one life over another is called a dualism. Here one is giving a hypothetical situation like: "You get into an auto accident. You have a child and a dog in a car. You can only save one life. Whom do you save?" According to this logic, you always save the child, for the child is more rational than a dog. This is the logic behind speciesism (favoring humans over animals). This is also the logic behind Princeton animal ethicist Peter Singer's controversial "Argument from Marginal Cases (AMC)" where he argues that some animals are more rational than some humans such as peoples in comas, infants under a year old, and humans with intellectual disabilities. When having to choose between saving a highly intelligent dog and saving an intellectual impaired child with an intellectual disability, it would not be speciesist to save the dog over the child, for "reason" not "species membership" is the criterion for moral consideration (Salomon, 2010, "From Marginal Cases to Linked Oppressions").

Social Justice does not necessitate that rational capacity be a perquisite for receiving moral consideration or acting ethically and morally. Social justice is giving everyone what they need and some of what they want to survive and flourish, regardless of their functioning abilities. Everyone then is expected to contribute to society as they are able and take only their fair share, so everyone gets social justice through costs/benefits being distributed equitably.

Conflict resolution, acknowledges individual dignity and agency which is often missing in social justice. This is because, conflict resolution refuses to choose between lives, which conflict resolution contends is an unnecessary "win-lose" solution which perpetuates injustice and violence, when a "win-win" solution is possible through the right balancing. Such as privileging people over things and coming up with solutions which gives everyone social justice. Both approaches take seriously empirical truths as a legitimate ethical-moral category.

The implications for the animal and disability movements cannot be understated. Not only are all peoples with disabilities and all animals entitled to social justice, but even the ecological whole is entitled to social justice, addressing disconnects with the environmental movements too. Justice is made possible through engaging conflict resolution processes like negotiation, reconciliation, mediation, arbitration, coalition building, and nonviolent communication. Some religious traditions even contend that some of their mystics have been able to engage in direct, unmediated interspecies conflict resolution with other animal species, so this model could also be applied to animal-human conflicts directly like wildlife-human conflicts in the suburbs or disputes with your own animal companion.

In other words, what I have provided is a crip neurodiverse argument for animal liberation based on social and environmental justice, interest-based conflict resolution, ecological holism, feminist communitarianism, and urban studies.

This is the summation of my argument from neurodiversity: The ecoability movements get beyond "poster children" like Grandin and protesting ableism in the People for the Ethical Treatment of Animals (PETA) and turn our attention to collaborating and coalition-building with the animal liberation movements to develop a mixed-methodology approach, a qualitative-quantitative approach, to "enacting civic engagement and social transformation" on behalf of all animal kind where we play an active visible role both participating in and helping to lead the animal liberation movements.

References

4-JCAS-Vol-VIII-Issue-I-and-II-2010-Essay-FROM-MARGINAL-CASES-pp-47-72.pdf. (n.d.). Retrieved April 10, 2020, from http://www.criticalanimalstudies.org/wp-content/uploads/2009/09/4-JCAS-Vol-VIII-Issue-I-and-II-2010-Essay-FROM-MARGINAL-CASES-pp-47-72.pdf. Many citations and references for this chapter can be found in my 2010 Journal of Critical Animal Studies Article (JCAS) "From Marginal Cases to Linked Oppressions: Reframing the Conflict between the Autistic Pride and Animal Rights Movements."

Ad Hominem Arguments—Douglas Walton—Google Books. (n.d.). Retrieved April 10, 2020, from https://books.google.com/books?id=48zCDAAAQBAJ&printsec=frontcover&dq=ad+hominem+fallacy&hl=en&newbks=1&newbks_redir=0&sa=X&ved=2ahUKEwiGkMa5ld7oAhXH854KHfKdBcUQ6AEwAHoECAIQAg#v=onepage&q=ad%20hominem%20fallacy&f=false. *Ad Hominem* arguments are considered a logical fallacy in academic philosophy (attacking a person instead of their ideas) yet are used frequently in the popular media and politics.

After the Protests Are Heard: Enacting Civic Engagement and Social ... - Sharon D. Welch—Google Books. (n.d.). Retrieved April 10, 2020, from https://books.google.com/books?id=Sol5DwAAQBAJ&printsec=frontcover&dq=sharon+welch+AND+after+the+protests+are+heard&hl=en&newbks=1&newbks_redir=0&sa=X&ved=2ahUKEwjlrIui3t7oAhUDnZ4KHUumCBIQ6AEwAHoECAQQAg#v=onepage&q=sharon%20welch%20AND%20after%20the%20protests%20are%20heard&f=false. Welch is a Unitarian Universalist (UU) social ethicist, feminist theorist, religious studies scholar, and an anti-racist advocate. She has devoted her life to putting feminist theory in dialogue with critical race theory and critical theory for the purpose of qualitative analysis, mutual critique, advocacy, and practice. She believes that confronting the history of racial inequity in America is the key to effectively addressing other social justice concerns in America because white racism has "shaped and formed" American society and culture.

An Analysis of Factors Related to Receipt of Accommodations and Services by Postsecondary Students with Disabilities—Lynn A. Newman, Joseph W. Madaus, 2015. (2015). https://journals-sagepub-com.proxy.lib.pdx.edu/doi/full/10.1177/0741932515572912. Provides statistics with data analysis which supports the notion that most Americans with disabilities cannot do what Grandin did—accommodate ourselves.

An Autistic Activist Responds To Temple Grandin | Our Compass. (n.d.). Retrieved April 10, 2020, from https://our-compass.org/2014/01/30/an-autistic-activist-responds-to-temple-grandin/. Jim Sinclair is the author of the article.

Animals, Disability, and the End of Capitalism: Voices from the Eco-ability ... - Google Books. (2019). https://books.google.com/books?id=IKJNuQEACAAJ&dq=%22Animals,+Disability+and+the+End+of+Capitalism%22&hl=en&newbks=1&newbks_redir=0&sa=X&ved=2ahUKEwjBoIL9qpvmAhUXFTQIHU-yC_cQ6AEwAHoECAMQAg. See for a greater diversity of ability voices beyond Grandin's background and views.

Animals in Translation: Using the Mysteries of Autism to Decode Animal Behavior—Temple Grandin, Catherine Johnson—Google Books. (n.d.). Retrieved April 10, 2020, from https://books.google.com/books?id=1WUg8XnuL-wC&printsec=frontcover&dq=Grandin+Animals+In+Translation&hl=en&newbks=1&newbks_redir=0&sa=X&ved=2ahUKEwjR_PG_1N7oAhVVip4KHZVpCmsQ6AEwAXoECAgQAg#v=onepage&q=Grandin%20Animals%20In%20Translation&f=false. Book which this chapter draws from.

Animals Make Us Human: Creating the Best Life for Animals—Temple Grandin, Catherine Johnson—Google Books. (n.d.). Retrieved April 10, 2020, from https://books.google.com/books?id=7ROWAAAAQBAJ&printsec=frontcover&dq=Grandin&hl=en&newbks=1&newbks_redir=0&sa=X&ved=2ahUKEwiY_ZGi1N7oAhXZGDQIHUrtBEsQ6AEwA3oECAYQAg#v=onepage&q=Grandin&f=false. Book which this chapter draws from.

Asperger's Children: The Origins of Autism in Nazi Vienna—Edith Sheffer—Google Books. (2018). https://books.google.com/books?id=7MM6DwAAQBAJ&printsec=frontcover&dq=%22Asperger%27s+Children%22&hl=en&newbks=1&newbks_redir=0&sa=X&ved=2ahUKEwjip6T1q5vmAhWQvJ4KHZW6A2IQ6AEwAHoECAYQAg#v=onepage&q=%22Asperger's%20Children%22&f=false. Hans Asperger whom the Asperger diagnosis is named after was a pediatrician, medical theorist and professor, and Nazi collaborator in Vienna, Austria, who was able to save the lives of individuals on the autism spectrum which he saw as high functioning. Those deemed high-functioning individuals were subjected to violent abusive behavioral interventions in the effort to make them of use and functional in Nazi society. Those deemed low functioning were turned over the Nazi's to be brutally murdered. The high-functioning survivors came out of his program with very serious trauma issues while Asperger went off to have a very successful career in psychiatry until 1979 when he passed away. Sounds familiar! Sheffer, the German historian of this study, wants to empower the neurodiversity movement by helping us to understand how over identifying with our diagnosis could lead to activating bias and stigma, e.g., separating people into "high" and "low" functioning. Sheffer even claims that the word "Asperger" now has stigma attached to it.

Beasts of Burden: Animal and Disability Liberation—Sunaura Taylor—Google Books. (2017). https://books.google.com/books?id=akc2DgAAQBAJ&printsec=frontcover&dq=beasts+of+burden&hl=en&newbks=1&newbks_redir=0&sa=X&ved=2ahUKEwjFpqrXq5vmAhXEl54KHYRyDxUQ6AEwAHoECAUQAg#v=onepage&q=beasts%20of%20burden&f=false. Crip animal activist who is a vegan and abolitionist and has written about my 2020 JACS article.

Developing Talents: Careers for Individuals with Asperger Syndrome and High . . . - Temple Grandin, Kate Duffy—Google Books. (n.d.). Retrieved April 10, 2020, from https://books.google.com/books?id=OH0iV7Z0VogC&printsec=frontcover&dq=Grandin+Talents&hl=en&newbks=1&newbks_redir=0&sa=X&ved=2ahUKEwjV_qPc-1N7oAhVPqZ4KHDdiwCO0Q6AEwAHoECAUQAg#v=onepage&q=Grandin%20Talents&f=false. Book which I draw from for this chapter.

Heterogeneous Trajectories of Depressive Symptoms in Late Middle Age: Critical Period, Accumulation, and Social Mobility Life Course Perspectives—Eunsun Kwon, BoRin Kim, Hyunjoo Lee, Sojung Park, 2018. (n.d.). Retrieved December 4, 2019, from https://journals-sagepub-com.proxy.lib.pdx.edu/doi/full/10.1177/08982 64317704540. A study which provides statistics with data analysis and which documents the long-term psychological effects of being exposed to a lifetime of adversity.

In the Company of Rebels: A Generational Memoir of Bohemians, Deep Heads . . . - Chellis Glendinning—Google Books. (n.d.). Retrieved April 10, 2020, from https://books. google.com/books?id=IuadDwAAQBAJ&printsec=frontcover&dq=chellis+glen denning+AND+in+the+company+of+rebels&hl=en&newbks=1&newbks_redir= 0&sa=X&ved=2ahUKEwjVs8HA3t7oAhXUsZ4KHTdmAsoQ6AEwAHoECAQ QAg#v=onepage&q=chellis%20glendenning%20AND%20in%20the%20comp any%20of%20rebels&f=false. Glendinning's latest book.

Interpreting Straw Man Argumentation: The Pragmatics of Quotation and Reporting—Fabrizio Macagno, Douglas Walton—Google Books. (n.d.). Retrieved April 10, 2020, from https://books.google.com/books?id=Sq80DwAAQBAJ&printsec=frontco ver&dq=inauthor:%22Fabrizio+Macagno%22&hl=en&newbks=1&newbks_redir= 0&sa=X&ved=2ahUKEwi_-OLblt7oAhXQJTQIHRXwDaQQ6AEwAnoECAM QAg#v=onepage&q&f=false. *Straw man arguments* are considered logically fallacies in academic philosophy, yet are frequently used in popular media and politics.

Intersectionality of Critical Animal Studies: A Historical Collection—Google Books. (n.d.). Retrieved December 3, 2019, from https://books.google.com/books?id=KwXlw QEACAAJ&dq=%22Intersectionality+of+Critical+Animal+Studies:+A+Historical+ Collection%22&hl=en&newbks=1&newbks_redir=0&sa=X&ved=2ahUKEwi40v jAq5vmAhWBrJ4KHYkFC-4Q6AEwAHoECAEQAg. A more expansive representative sample of ability backgrounds, voices, and views on animal issues.

John Dao & Rebeeca Roberts. (n.d.). *Liberation science: Putting science to work for social and environmental justice—Steven H. Emerman, Marcia Bjørnerud, Jill S. Schneiderman, Sarah A. Levy—Google Books.* Retrieved December 3, 2019, from https://books.google.com/books?hl=en&lr=&id=EmYDBAAAQBAJ&oi= fnd&pg=PA3&dq=%22Bisphenol+A:+Mothers+Shouldn%27t+have+to+be+Scienti sts%22&ots=qAlen0vuPK&sig=0VADBYXsw2HOuvNVDMBL--SJOf4#v=onep age&q=%22Bisphenol%20A%3A%20Mothers%20Shouldn't%20have%20to%20 be%20Scientists%22&f=false. A collection of essays showing what is possible in terms of effecting social and environmental justice within the constraints of mixed research methods (quantitative-qualitative).

Kruse, C. R. (2001). The movement and the media: Framing the debate over animal experimentation. *Political Communication*, *18*(1), 67–87. https://doi.org/10.1080/ 10584600150217668

Open Intro Statistics—Create Space Independent Publishing Platform, from http://lean-pub.com/openintro-statistics

Phallacies: Historical Intersections of Disability and Masculinity—Google Books. (n.d.). Retrieved April 10, 2020, from https://books.google.com/books?hl=en&lr=&id=wWEwDwAAQBAJ&oi=fnd&pg=PP1&dq=disability+and+masculinity&ots=RDItpouP2o&sig=0zro5Gz-27qJE8WxndLQaBXkiKE#v=onepage&q=disability%20and%20masculinity&f=false. A collection of essays by historians providing historical documentation of how exactly patriarchy is repressive to disabled men (both physical and invisible).

Songs of the Gorilla Nation: My Journey through Autism—Dawn Prince-Hughes, Ph.D. - Google Books. (n.d.). Retrieved April 10, 2020, from https://books.google.com/books?id=h6lt_mzE58QC&printsec=frontcover&dq=Dawn-Prince-Hughes&hl=en&newbks=1&newbks_redir=0&sa=X&ved=2ahUKEwjt-cbU3d7oAhVMrp4KHVKnChkQ6AEwAHoECAYQAg#v=onepage&q=Dawn-Prince-Hughes&f=false.

The Archetype of the Ape-Man: The Phenomenological Archaeology of a Relic … - Dawn Prince-Hughes—Google Books. (n.d.-b). Retrieved April 10, 2020, from https://books.google.com/books?id=BriAUg2VTrEC&printsec=frontcover&dq=dawn+prince+hughes&hl=en&newbks=1&newbks_redir=0&sa=X&ved=2ahUKEwjp-ujs-3d7oAhVGsZ4KHfHECFEQ6AEwBHoECAMQAg#v=onepage&q=dawn%20prince%20hughes&f=false. Book based on Prince-Hughes doctor dissertation at the Universitat Herisau in Switzerland. An opportunity to go deeper and richer with her ideas and lifework.

The Autism Job Club: The Neurodiverse Workforce in the New Normal of Employment—Michael Bernick, Richard Holden—Google Books. (n.d.). Retrieved April 10, 2020, from https://books.google.com/books?id=ljaCDwAAQBAJ&pg=PT23&dq=%22Temple+Grandin%22+AND+%22the+new+normal%22&hl=en&newbks=1&newbks_redir=0&sa=X&ved=2ahUKEwjyy-Gh097oAhUKHDQIHSZLAqUQ6AEwAXoECAIQAg#v=onepage&q=%22Temple%20Grandin%22%20AND%20%22the%20new%20normal%22&f=false

Vanesa Castan Broto & Harriet Bulkeley. (n.d.). *Maintaining Climate Change Experiments: Urban Political Ecology and the Everyday Reconfiguration of Urban Infrastructure—Broto—2013—International Journal of Urban and Regional Research—Wiley Online Library.* Retrieved November 12, 2019, from https://onlinelibrary-wiley-com.proxy.lib.pdx.edu/doi/full/10.1111/1468-2427.12050. Go for background about the urban context for accessibility to ecological lifestyles.

Yasuyo Makido, Dana Hellman, & Vivek Shandas. (2019, March 30). *Nature based designs to mitigate urban heat—the efficiency of green infrastructure treatments in Portland, Oregon—USP-630-001: RESEARCH DESIGN (Fall 2019).* https://d2l.pdx.edu/d2l/le/content/765349/viewContent/4296635/View. Go for background about the urban context for accessibility to ecological lifestyles (Makido, Hellman, & Shandas, March, 2019).

3. Selection for *and* against Disability: Assistance Dogs

Birkan Taş

Introduction

From hunting to herding to guarding to emotional support, dogs have played a significant role in human civilization, commonly referred to as 'man's best friend.' As such, reflecting on human-canine bond mobilized interdisciplinary research across various fields such as anthropology, cultural studies, history, and feminist theory among others. For instance, a focus on the history of dog breeding helped researchers trace raced and classed relationships between humans and dogs in the European colonial context (Worboys et. al., 2018; Brandow, 2015). These accounts show that dogs played a special role in the separation of the ruling elite from everyone else, and of the "civilized" from the "uncivilized," which underpinned ideas about social differentiation and hierarchies based on gender, sexuality, race, and disability.

There is a small but growing literature on the intersection between critical animal studies and critical disability studies. This chapter builds on existing dialogic attempts to create a critical conversation between these two disciplines by focusing on assistance dogs, which are purpose-bred canines individually trained to perform specific tasks for people with disabilities. Example of such work includes 'guide dogs' helping blind or visually impaired people, 'hearing dogs' aiding people with hearing impairments, 'mobility assistance dogs' providing balance and stability, 'medical alert' or 'seizure dogs' providing assistance to people with various health conditions such as diabetes, and 'psychiatric service dogs' providing comfort and bringing medication during anxiety attacks. With the advancement of training programs—as well as selective breeding technologies—humans continue to attribute ever new "functions" to canines. For example, during the Covid-19 pandemic some "medical detection," also known as "bio-detection dogs," who could successfully detect malaria, were re-trained to detect the coronavirus by smell.

Assistance dogs have to experience months of extensive training starting in puppyhood when they have to learn to perform specific tasks and obey commands. The characteristics, fur, and size of the dogs determine their suitability to meet the needs of people with certain physical and mental disabilities. Therefore, certain breeds, such as golden retrievers, labrador retrievers and poodles, are said to be more suitable for being assistance dogs than others. If they are able to pass the training period, they are matched with a person or family as a working animal. Once their working life comes to an end, some of them are re-homed or sent to shelters, while others are euthanized if they are considered to be too old, ill, or unsuitable for re-homing.

Focusing on assistance dogs offers a fresh perspective to discuss the shared vulnerability of humans and dogs and their dependence on each other. In this chapter, I will criticize the myth of independence, which is a common trope in discussions around assistance dog services. Instead, I will argue that vulnerability is shared by human and nonhuman animals, and discuss the ways in which dependencies are socially, economically, and culturally produced. Rather than seeing vulnerability and dependence as mere obstacles that should be fought off with individual interventions, I will posit them as sites of connection, responsibility, and care. Moreover, focusing on the ways in which ideas about health and normalcy coalesce and play out in selective dog breeding can open up new ways of thinking and critiquing breed standards as an issue of race.

Breed Norms

Disability studies examines and undermines the ways norms surrounding bodies and minds are produced and reproduced over time. Disability scholar Lennard Davis writes that the idea of a norm appears in English over the period 1840–1860 in relation to statistics and eugenics in order to classify and govern populations (2006, p. 3). Modern nations were obsessed with identifying and governing individual bodies and making generalizations by placing the individual within a legible group. Norming populations through measuring "identificatory physical qualities" within a matrix of the "hegemony of the normal" marked certain bodies as normal and others as abnormal within a binary system. Bodies deemed abnormal were categorized and isolated, which led to forced sterilization, institutionalization, and mass murder of thousands of people with disabilities (Davis, pp. 7–12). .

In *Fantasies of identification: Disability, race, gender,* disability studies scholar Ellen Samuels writes that colonialism, urbanization, the beginning of the welfare state, and greater geographic mobility due to industrial revolution created anxieties about social identities, which resulted in a desire to name and classify people (2014, pp. 1–3). Samuels' intersectional analysis shows how race, gender, and disability intersected in modern nations during the mid-19th century to shape a "fantasy of identification," which "combine a certain wistful desire to know and understand certain identities with a persistent and often violent imposition of identity upon people whose subjectivity is overruled by a homogenizing, bureaucratic imperative" (p. 3). Placing an individual within a legible group was based on the rigidity of embodied social identities such as gender, race, and disability.

Samuels' analysis of the complex ways race, gender, class, and national identity mutually constitute each other during the 19th century is quite informative. She aims to show how the uncertainty of the category of disability resists classificatory systems but, nonetheless, provides the ground "to structure a system of identification that seeks to fix individual bodily identity" (p. 14). "As the trope of physicality," disability's symbolic function, based on the ideas of normal and natural, informed racial and gendered debates in the 19th century (pp. 14–15). If in Samuel's analysis fantasies of identification persist through mutual constitution of intersecting vectors of power, then examining the ways in which biologically distinct nonhuman bodies became fixed, visible, and legible though breed norms offers a new kind of intersectional analysis. The identification and categorization of animals play a vital element of the regulative and coercive discourse surrounding fantasies of identification, which she does not engage with. However, it is no coincidence that the concept of "normal" and dog shows as conformations to norms emerged during the same period. Dog shows are the prime examples of the masculinist desire that aims to render social identities as fixed and verifiable within a discourse of scientific racism and the authority of medicine. Thus, focusing on the way in which dog breeding and shows substantiate ideas about normalcy and standardization enriches analyses of how race, gender, and disability intersect.

Ideas around normal as "conforming to a type, standard or regular pattern" were strictly applied to breeds and especially pedigree dogs, who were categorized according to physical standards (Merriam-Webster, n.d.). Breed dogs and dog shows helped perpetuate fantasies of identification based on fixed and legible traits, which could be improved through training. If categorizing and fixing bodies as a form of social disciplining reflect a "crisis of identification" in relation to the "mutually entangled and constitutive dynamic of disability, gender, and race," pedigree dog breeding reflects the management of such a crisis par excellence (Samuel, 2014, p. 16). That is why reflecting on breed as a legible and fixed identity category based on physical standards and character norms is a disability issue insofar as reversing the hegemony of the normal and finding ways to rethink what counts as abnormal is a critical task for disability scholars (Davis, 2006, p. 15). Thus a dialogue between critical animal studies and critical disability studies perspectives is vital for an intersectional critique of normalcy.

Dog breeding is a gendered, raced, and classed mechanism of control of canine sexuality. Assistance dogs, as skilled workers, are the product of artificial insemination to meet human needs. The pervasive use of certain breeds as assistance dogs reflects this mechanism of social control, which reveals deeper issues about sexuality, personhood, and autonomy. The idea of good breeding, which dates back to 19th-century dog shows, is inseparable from eugenic ideas about respectable citizenship through breeding and training (Rasmussen, 2011). As Claire Rasmussen (2016) writes:

> Dog breeding emerges in a particular discursive context that indicated the interconnections between humans and animals. Understood as arising with scientific racism, evolutionary biology, the cult of domesticity, and processes of democratization, dog shows appear less as a frivolous amusement and more as a part of a political discourse about proper citizenship within a democratizing society marked by race, class, gender, and sexual difference. (78)

Ideas about lineage, bloodlines, purity, heredity, and biological traits of pedigree dogs emerged as a result of scientific racism in an effort to standardize human and nonhuman animal populations. The domestication and control of dog population through bloodlines was extended to other populations, which should be domesticated, tamed, or civilized within a system of racism, ableism, and colonialism. "Good bred" and trained dogs became symbols for national unity, loyalty, and obedience such as German shepherd dogs, which are identified with the Nazi regime. For that reason a critical animal studies perspective, which fights for the liberation of all animals, needs to be intersectional, as human interaction with nonhuman animals reveal the various ways in which sexuality, gender, race, nationality, and disability converge.

The eugenist discourse of scientific racism is not a matter of the past but survives in the present in new forms. The perfectly behaved canines who experience one-and-a-half or two years of training need to show no anxiety, cope with stress, get used to disturbing sounds, be confident and hardworking, and have no impairment. That is why the modern invention of dog breeding is a disability issue, in which ideas about normalcy converge at the level of appearance, character, training, and discipline. To put it differently, dog breeding is shaped by and shapes ideas about normalcy and docility through regulative discourses and training. The pervasiveness of inbreeding to raise a standardized trait results in a reduced gene pool that causes breed-specific disabilities. For instance, many large-size breeds are prone to hip dysplasia. Dachshunds are more likely to have back problems than any other breed. French Bulldogs are susceptible to breathing problems and their increased skull size due to inbreeding prevent them from giving birth naturally and make them dependent on human intervention in order to survive. Breed dogs are "simultaneously disabled and hyperabled" through "very enhancements that make them especially profitable to industries and desirable to consumers," as Sunaura Taylor writes in *Beast of Burden: Animal and disability liberation* (2017, p. 39).

The various ways in which assistance dogs are categorized, standardized, and exploited expose the intricate relationship between ableism and speciesism. The notion of independence could illuminate this intricate relationship. Many legal documents, such as the Americans with Disabilities Act (2010) and assistance dog institutions, state that assistance dogs increase the independence of people with disabilities by mitigating their disability-related limitations. Reduced to prosthetic devices or mere tools serving for human purposes, the well-being of dogs, which are individually trained, sold, retired, and denied play and affection during work time, is of secondary importance in such legal documents. Situating assistance dogs not as passive objects or mere tools but co-producers of interspecies relationships, yet entangled in an asymmetrical interdependence, is necessary to disrupt speciest ideologies in discourses surrounding disability.

The Myth of Independence as a Form of Speciesism

The idea that assistance dogs help people with disabilities achieve greater independence persists even though the relationship is a form of interdependence and animal exploitation. The supposition that a disabled person becomes more independent by acquiring an assistance dog pervades contemporary representations of assistance dogs, which render them as invisible caregivers within a speciest economy. This logic is predicated on negating and overlooking "dog's existence as a separate being," in which human life is given more value over nonhuman lives (Edminster, 2011, p. 133). Dogs are treated as commodities whose invisible labor and care work are ignored within a discourse of speciesism and ableism, based on strict distinctions between humans and nonhuman animals, and between normal and abnormal.

The myth of independence is embedded in an animal welfare paradigm, which focuses on reducing pain, stress, and suffering of animals rather than promoting their right to live without human intervention. Ethical breeding or humane treatment of animals operate within a system marked by racial, classed, gendered, speciest, and ableist distinctions, which serve for the instrumentalization of animal suffering and exploitation. The rights and welfare framework is based on an ideology that values nonhuman animals less than humans, which justify their instrumentalization and use for human ends.

The instrumentalization of assistance dogs as functional prosthetics and skilled professionals for human independence subordinates animals to human needs. Emerged in English in the 18th-century medical texts, prosthetics conventionally meant as replacements for missing limbs. According to David Serlin, following World War II, prosthetics operated within "the fiercely heterosexual culture of rehabilitation medicine, especially its orthodox zeal to preserve the masculine status of disabled veterans" (as cited in Shildrick, 2017, p. 139). Thus, prosthetics emerged "to re-normalize the disabled [heterosexual] male body" (Ibid., p. 139). Margrit Schildrick notes that the success of prosthetics "was often measured in professional literature by the extent to which they enabled the wearer to engage in normal gender activities" (2017, p. 139). In other words, approximating an image of a nondisabled body through rehabilitation and prosthetics is historically embedded in approximating and reclaiming masculinity and heterosexuality.

During a research trip to an assistance dog center in Belgium, I interviewed a wheelchair user who was living with her fourth assistance dog, a golden retriever. He would help her get out of the bed, open the doors, help her undress, retrieve objects, pick up the phone, empty the mailbox, etc. The tasks that she requires from her dog such as picking an object from the floor would be extremely repetitive and boring for humans. That is why she would not prefer a human assistant doing the same tasks as an assistance dog does. She believes that compared to humans, dogs do not have any hidden agendas and would never betray humans, which makes them better caregivers. When I asked her about her take on independence, she said that an assistance dog would give her "a feeling of more independence" even though she would still be dependent on other people for some tasks that her dog could not perform. Yet, nowhere in the conversation, she mentioned her dependence on the dog.

The training school where she met the dog would only train labradors and golden retrievers with a "decent bloodline" and without any diseases, as she put it. As the epitome of "successful" breeding, golden retrievers and labrador retrievers are favored for their size, intelligence, sociability, and trainability. Yet many of them develop cancer later in their lives or have knee and elbow problems due to inbreeding as the trainer of the school explained to me in another interview. My talk with the trainer revealed that many dogs with a so-called reliable bloodline have medical issues starting from puppyhood, which becomes harder to monitor. Insofar as, historically, the appearance of a dog in comparison to an idealized norm has been the primary criteria for breed standards (ear shape, fur color, skull size, etc.), breed dogs reflect the detrimental effect of human control of animal sexuality. Thus, the common sense assumption that "purebred" dogs are healthier than mutts obscure the fact that many breeds develop breed-specific diseases due to a limited gene pool, and it is used to justify human control of animal sexuality for exploiting animal labor for human needs.

Can we understand relations of instrumentality between people with disabilities and assistance dogs other than speciesism? Can training animals operate within a space of mutual respect and communication? I doubt so. A successful assistance dog has to conform to certain normative character-istics and obey commands. Breeding and training dogs to perform certain tasks for human needs is a violent act of human control over a dog's sexuality and character. That is why more intersectional analysis is needed for animal and disability liberation, which examines how sexuality, gender, race, and disability intersect in the treatment of nonhuman animals by humans.

When confronted with the question about the well-being of assistance dogs, many users or trainers say that compared to pet dogs assistance dogs are happier because they can spend more time outside home while helping their guardians and can enjoy the freedom to enter into places, which are denied to pets. For example, when I asked my ethnographic informant about the difference between an assistance dog and a human caregiver in terms of consent, and whether humans have the right to use dogs for human purposes she told me that her dog "likes" working. Yet this assumption is based on an anthropomorphic idea, which does not take into account the objectification and oppression of dogs and impose a vague idea of happiness. A "better-off-than-pet" approach is commonly used to justify violence against assistance dogs within a welfarist perspective, which is predicated upon a strict divide between humans and dogs, and the superiority of humans.

The trainer I interviewed with during my research visit in Belgium men-tioned the importance of telling her clients to keep in mind the question, "how can your dog be a dog?" which she relates to meeting the needs of dogs before expecting them to perform certain tasks. "How can a dog be a dog?" is an important question that can be extended to other species. The question cannot be thought apart from the human expectation of normative behav-iors from nonhuman animals. Leaving aside fantasies of identification, which aim to control and homogenize species, breeds, and people with disabilities, could be an important step toward the liberation of animals and people with disabilities.

Interspecies Care

Rather than being a unidirectional practice, especially feminist, queer, and crip accounts on the politics of care suggest that care is best understood as the product or outcome of the relationship between two or more people, enmeshed in unequal power relations. As an issue of social justice, care operates not only as a site of connectedness, and mutual help, but also neglect, and dispossession. Thus, focusing on the dynamics and different modalities of care reveal the operation of inequality and exploitation as some bodies are worthy objects of care and rehabilitation while others are denied access. For that reason, the question why care is inseparable from the question how to care?

Care relations are increasingly privatized, quantified, and commodified. Those who are in power decide how to care about and take care of whereas those with less power deal with care-giving and care-receiving. For that reason rethinking care provides an important ground to develop new forms of critique, organization, policy making, community building, and intersectional analyses. Politicizing care relationships at both caregiving and care-receiving levels is an important path for animal and disability liberation.

Care relations can be unidirectional and patronizing without taking into consideration the needs of human and nonhuman animals. Thinkers and activists in disability studies criticize forms of care that are individualized and universal that do not take into consideration care as a form of community building and as contingent. Scholars in disability studies criticize care being turned into charity and instead argue for an institutional form of care that is available for everyone. Feminist ethics of care criticizes the ways in which care relations are feminized and devalued due to their link to connection, intimacy, and dependency. A masculinist worldview which praises autonomy and independence distances itself from care relations as a feminized work. What does caring for nonhuman animals mean for critical animal studies?

Caring is a necessary component to bring social justice to human and nonhuman animals. It requires finding ways to listen to voices and needs of animals and seeing the intersectionality of oppressions by refusing to choose between caring for animals and caring for humans. Within the context of assistance dog services, caring requires rethinking forms of dependencies not mere obstacles, but a condition of becoming albeit allocated differently.

Ableist ideas surrounding independence as an attainable goal need to be debunked by an intersectional analysis, which opposes "all forms of instrumentalization, commodification, and exploitation of both non-human and human animals" (Weisberg, 2014, p. 110)

Breeding animals for human needs raises questions about the visibility and invisibility of disability. Insofar as assistance dogs are bred to be healthy and conform to norms that reflect anthropocentric ideologies, breeding is an important site to examine how ideas about normalcy, race, and ability operate contemporary capitalist exploitation of animals and people with disabilities. As Taylor notes:

> We need to crip animal ethics, incorporating a disability politics into the ways we think about animals. It is essential that we examine the shared systems and ideologies that oppress both disabled humans and nonhuman animals, because ableism perpetuates animal oppression in more areas than the linguistic. Indeed, ableism is intimately entangled with speciesism, and is deeply relevant to thinking through the ways nonhuman animals are judged, categorized, and exploited. (57)

Cripping selective dog breeding for disabled people requires how norms around animal personality and character is detrimental to the flourishing of animals. Cripping contests compulsory ableism and the ways in which it is selectively (re)produced, naturalized, and made invisible. Crip practices aim to create coalitional politics and solidarity by opening dialogue between queer studies, critical race studies, feminist theory, class analysis, and transsexual studies, among others. In this context, crip theory and practices aim to open a space for alternative presents and futures for disability studies by pushing boundaries and going beyond identity politics. To this end, an intersectional analysis and abolitionist politics, which refuses a binary opposition between humans and animals, is necessary in order to fight against infantilizing and universal care relations. Cripping critical animal studies requires attending to the complex ways in which dependencies are produced and reproduced through ableist and speciesist ideologies. Politicizing dependencies, rejecting a masculinist world view that values independence over interdependence, provides a common ground care for human and nonhuman animals.

Dependencies and vulnerabilities are irreducible conditions of being in the world. Politicizing vulnerability and (inter)dependence and their value, and how they are allocated differently across bodies, species, and geographies can help us resist the individualized and commercialized care relations within contemporary neoliberal capitalism in order to fight for total liberation of human and nonhuman animals. In their special relation to dependency and disability, which is both hypervisible and invisible, assistance dogs show us the importance of politicizing vulnerability and interdependence and their value in our lives in order to resist the individualizing, commercializing, and monetizing ideologies, which frame dependency and disability as negative and abnormal. Interspecies care requires abolishing **speciesist** and ableist ideologies that are ingrained in the social fabric of capitalist economy. In this context veganism can be thought as a form of interspecies care, insofar as the exploitation of nonhuman animals provides one of the pillars of the capitalist economic structure, which is a system based on institutional racism, sexism, and speciesism. For that reason human and nonhuman liberation needs to be anti-capitalist, anti-sexist, and anti-speciesist.

Neoliberal capitalism, which is based on the accumulation of profit and exploitation of nature, continues to create new debilities and has caused the extinction of many species of animals. In this context, an intersectional analysis of disability studies and animal studies is crucial in order to create breathable presents and futures for nonhuman and human animals. Ableist and speciesist comparisons between the cognitive capacity of people with disabilities and animals that continue to frame many debates in animal rights discourses make it necessary to analyze the complex ways in which ability and animality interact. A critical animal studies perspective rejects any form of objectification, exploitation, and commodification of human and nonhuman lives. Its criticality refers to addressing the urgency of the effects of ecological destruction and the need for addressing the intersectionality of oppression by dismantling speciesist ideologies. This is crucial to change structures of domination and rethink what dependence, independence, and interdependence mean.

"If animal and disability oppression are entangled, might not that mean their paths of liberation are entangled as well?" (Taylor, 2017, p. xv). This path of liberation can be based on politicizing dependency, criticizing the myth of independence as a measure of responsible citizenship, bringing to the fore care relations between human and animal studies, and thinking about veganism as practicing interspecies care and justice in everyday life.

References

Brandow, M. (2015). *A matter of breeding: A biting history of pedigree dogs and how the quest for status has harmed man's best friend*. Beacon Press.

Davis, L. (2006). *The disability studies reader* (2nd ed.). Routledge.

Edminster, A. (2011). Interspecies families, freelance dogs, and personhood: Saved lives and being one at an assistance dog agency. In L. Kalof, & G. M. Montgomery (Eds.), *Making animal meaning* (pp. 127–143). Michigan State University Press.

Merriam-Webster. (n.d.). Semantics. In Merriam-Webster.com dictionary. Retrieved May 10, 2020, from https://www.merriam-webster.com/dictionary/normal

Rasmussen, C. (2016). Domesticating bodies: Race, species, sex, and citizenship. In J. Grant, & V. Jungkunz (Eds.), *Political theory and the animal/human relationship* (pp. 75–101). State University of New York Press.

Samuels, E. (2014). *Fantasies of identification: Disability, gender, race*. New York UP.

Shildrick, M. (2017). Border crossings: The technology of disability and desire. In A. Waldschmidt, H. Berressem, & M. Ingwersen (Eds.), *Culture, theory, disability: Encounters between disability studies and cultural studies* (pp. 137–151). Transcript.

Taylor, S. (2017). *Beasts of burden: Animal and disability liberation*. The New Press.

Weisberg, Z. (2014). The trouble with posthumanism: Bacteria are people too. In J. Sorenson (Ed.), *Critical animal studies: Thinking the unthinkable* (pp. 93–116). Canadian Scholars' Press Inc.

Worboys, M., Strange J. M., & Pemberton, N. (2018). *The invention of the modern dog: Breed and blood in victorian britain*. Johns Hopkins University Press.

4. Queering the Animate Body: Toxicity, Ecoability, and Multispecies Solidarity in Duplin County, North Carolina

Z. ZANE MCNEILL AND REBECCA ELI LONG

Introduction

Duplin County, North Carolina, confines more than 18.5 million animals in Concentrated Animal Feeding Operations (CAFOs), more commonly known as factory farms. Residents near CAFOs complain of the smell and report headaches, stomach pains, anxiety, and depression. Factory workers, meanwhile, face high levels of Post Traumatic Stress Disorder and workplace injury (Human Rights Watch, 2005; Leibler et al., 2017). Workers at hog CAFOs in nearby Bladen County report chronic muscle and nerve pain in addition to workplace accidents. As one worker explains, "What they want to know is, can you still work without bleeding in the meat?" (Dominic P. qtd. in Human Rights Watch, 2019, p. 27). Hogs are brought in, stunned, and bled out. The scene in one CAFO is grimly mechanized:

> Blood runs onto the floor as severed hogs' heads float overhead, hooked onto conveyor belts. The bodies move down the lines, the organs are removed, and the empty carcasses are sawed in half, beginning the disassembly that will end in hams, pork chops, and chitlins. (Waltz, 2018)

As Eli Claire has said, "locating the problems of social injustice in the world, rather than in our bodies, has been key to naming oppression" (Clare, 2001, p. 360). Factory farms in Duplin County and the surrounding area, considered part of the South's "Black Belt" region, have contaminated local water and air supplies, causing human illness, such as "blue baby syndrome." This leads to what Sunaura Taylor terms "ecological disablement"—a condition where the functioning of the entire ecosystem is impaired (2019).

Ecoability acknowledges multispecies relationships and encourages us to respect and value interrelationship, interconnectedness, and interdependence (Nocella II et al., 2012a, p. xiv). In this chapter, we examine the conditions that cause ecological disablement through the lens of toxicity.

Toxins contaminate what is considered the "normal" body, effectively disabling and queering the normative. They threaten common notions of rural farming, overtake communities, and eventually overwhelm the body of those who work and live near CAFOs. Thus "environmental toxicity and environmental degradation are figured as slow and dreadful threats" to the cisheteropatriarchal white supremacist State, while also offering marginalized communities, the environment, and nonhuman animals as sacrifice to capitalist growth (Chen, 2012, p. 7).

By understanding Duplin county, the environment itself, and the bodies of its inhabitants as queer, we are able to imagine a futurity that prioritizes ecoability, consistent anti-oppression, and disability, queer, and animal liberation. This chapter expands the link between disability and animal rights to explore how animal farming is itself a disabling practice and how there are avenues of resistance in the toxic body—a space to trouble notions of the fit/unfit paradigm, subvert capitalist notions of productivity, and offer new ways to understand the non/human body (Haraway, 2016).

By re-orienting Duplin county through the frameworks of queer ecologies and ecoability, it can become a "site[] of resistance...in the service of queer possibilities" (Erickson & Mortimer-Sandilands, 2010, p. 22). In doing so, we create a new framework to think through disability, animal rights, and environmentalism that fights against industrialized farming and the capitalist food regime as a whole.

Duplin County, NC: "Hog Hell"

The division between farmer and neighbor is palpable here—and falls along racial lines in a state where agriculture has its roots in the plantation system, and where Confederate monuments still stand on the Capitol's grounds (Buford, 2018).

Duplin County, described as "America's top hog-producing county . . . where future hams outnumber humans about 30 to 1" (Clark, 2018), is one of several counties in eastern North Carolina with a large population of hogs housed on CAFOs. This region is widely considered part of the South's Black Belt region and is also home to a growing Hispanic population and the Lumbee Tribe (Sturgis, 2017). A University of North Carolina Study found that these communities of color are between 1.39 and 2.18 times more likely to live within 3 miles of a CAFO (Wing & Johnston, 2014), a clear example of environmental injustice.

In Duplin County, approximately 4,660 residences housing an estimated 12,489 people—more than a fifth of the county's population—are located within a half-mile of a factory farm or manure pit.[1] Animal waste is routinely used as fertilizer and sprayed on crops. This waste contains dangerous toxins, including antibiotic-resistant bacteria, heavy metals, and greenhouse gasses (Marks, 2001). The odor, described as "reminiscent of rotten eggs and ammonia" (Nicole, 2013) and like a "body that's been decomposed for a month" (Yeoman, 2019), pervades the air and sometimes seeps into homes. Some days, everything outside is sprayed with a fine coating of manure (Nicole, 2013). Living in close proximity to toxins has a devastating effect on residents' health. One study of eastern North Carolina residents shows exposure to the odors of hog processing caused an increase in tension, anger, depression, fatigue, and confusion (Schiffman et al., 1995). Another study in the *North Carolina Medical Journal* found that communities located near CAFOs have higher rates of infant mortality, anemia, kidney disease, and tuberculosis (Kravchenko et al., 2018).

One resident, Rene Miller says:

> Mostly everybody in this neighborhood got asthma or even cancer. My neighbor there died from cancer probably just last year. My nephew down the street, he's got cancer. He's in terminal cancer stage four. Not a smoker, not a drinker. And it's not in his lungs. It's in his lymph nodes.[2]

Sacoby Wilson, an environmental health professor at the University of Maryland, says that the effects of hog farm pollution go well beyond noxious odors:

> You have exposures through air, water, and soil. You have ... inhalation, ingestion, and dermal exposures. People have been exposed to multiple chemicals: hydrogen sulfide, particulate matter, endotoxins, nitrogenous compounds. Then you have a plume that moves; what gets into the air gets into the water. You have runoff from spray fields. These are complex exposure profiles.[3]

The toxins from hog slaughter leech into the earth and become incorporated into the environment. In addition to atmospheric pollution from greenhouse gas emissions and fecal particulates, toxins impact ground and surface water. This can have drastic impacts on the ecosystem, including overgrowth of bacteria, death of aquatic life, and unsafe drinking water (Marks, 2001). These effects are not limited to Duplin County. Once the toxins reach the water system, they travel downstream, soon making their way to the Atlantic Ocean.

Runoff and related problems are especially profound during hurricane season. When North Carolina is hit with a major hurricane (such as Hurricane Florence in 2018, Hurricane Matthew in 2016, and Hurricane Floyd in 1999) hogs often drown. During Hurricane Floyd, more than 100,000 hogs drowned, leaving their carcasses to float downriver the ocean, along with hog feces (Formuzis, 2016). In the aftermath of these hurricanes, E. coli levels spike in public wells, compromising the safety of drinking water (Murawski, 2018). As extreme weather events increase and strong hurricanes become more frequent, such events could become regular, allowing little time for communities in eastern North Carolina to recover before another storm arrives.

In 2018, Hurricane Florence hit North Carolina with damaging winds and 8 trillion gallons of water (Buford, 2018), causing the deaths of over 20 people and 24 billion in economic damages (Duncan, 2019). North Carolina was ill equipped to handle the flooding caused by Florence. Hog waste from these CAFOs, kept in cesspools euphemistically called "lagoons" outside of the facilities, flooded, leaking into the local waterways (Pierre-Louis, 2018). The leakage of these lagoons caused algal blooms and the decimation of the fish population, in addition to unsafe drinking water for human consumption and a rise in "blue baby syndrome," a syndrome caused by a lack of oxygen and heart defects (Pierre-Louis, 2018).

In addition to contributing to the death of millions of hogs and pigs throughout North Carolina, CAFOs generate toxins that contaminate the air and ground water. The public health and environmental impacts are wide ranging. People living near these CAFOs report a litany of health concerns, including headaches, runny noses, sore throats, excessive coughing, respiratory problems, nausea, diarrhea, dizziness, burning eyes, depression, and fatigue (Marks, 2001, p. 1). Workers are exposed to dangerous and deadly conditions. Seepage from the lagoons pollutes groundwater and threatens aquatic life. The atmospheric deposition of ammonia that is emitted from lagoons and spray fields affects watersheds as far as 300 miles away (Marks, 2001, p. 2).

The health and environmental risks connected to the CAFOs have been "the subject of litigation, investigations, legislation and regulation" (Hellerstein & Fine, 2017). Multiple policy groups and NGOs, like Rural Empowerment Association for Community Help (REACH), Waterkeeper Alliance, and the NC Environmental Justice Network, continue to monitor the pollutants, focusing mostly on monitoring air quality (Sorg, 2020). Since 2014, more than two dozen lawsuits concerning lagoons and pig waste have been filed against Smithfield, a pork producer in the county (Yeoman, 2019).

These actions were primarily taken by the minority communities impacted. Plaintiffs have often won these cases, with damage awards from $102,400 to $473.5 million.[4]

Lily Kuo (July 14, 2014), a Quartz journalist, described the slew of lawsuits targeting pork producers as:

> The lawsuits mark the latest chapter in a decades-long battle. To outsiders, it may look like little more than a spat between neighbors. But at heart, it's a story about poverty and racial inequality, and how those forces play out in a state where the hog industry has emerged as both essential for the economy and an oppressor of poorer communities of color (2015).

At the heart of questions of poverty and racial inequality is ableism, defined as "systemic oppression [that] leads to people and society determining who is valuable or worthy based on people's appearance and/or their ability to satisfactorily produce, excel & 'behave'" (Lewis, 2019). People of Color (POC) have historically been understood to be deviant and deficient (Erevelles, 2014). This has exacerbated marginality and conditions that foster disability through impoverishment and violence. Working in and living near CAFOs is one such site of capitalist violence wrought on devalued bodies. Nonhuman animal bodies are also devalued and subjected to violence. The ecoability movement offers a chance to discuss these connected, but not identical, forms of violence, and their broader impacts on the environment.

Queer Ecologies, Animacies, and Ecoability

> Let me begin with my body, my disabled queer body. I use the word *queer* in both of its meanings: in general sense, as odd, quirky, not belonging...my first experience of queerness centered not on sexuality or gender, but on disability (Clare, 2001, p. 361).

Ecoability engages with histories of colonial, capitalist domination that position a certain type of human as superior and independent from the environment. This is constructed as "normal." This idea of normal is so pervasive that it becomes difficult to imagine alternatives. "Our subjectivities are so entangled with the discourses of Western industrial culture that many feel compelled to publicly concede to its legitimacy despite how it contributes to pervasive exploitation" (Lupinacci & Lupinacci, 2017, p. 63). Queer studies, disability studies, and ecoability decenter a normative subject and envision ways of building multispecies, connected communities.

In decentering the normative human subject, we reemphasize that humanity is a small part of nature, not separate from it. Embodiments, including disability, are also connected to and created by environmental interactions. Such an understanding builds on Alison Kafer's "political/relational model" of disability, which positions " 'disability' as a set of practices and associations that can be critiqued, contested, and transformed" (2013, p. 9). Recognizing the political/relational aspects of disability can reveal the inequalities that concentrate disabled ecologies in certain places. The category of "disability" as it engages with racism and classism opens the way for further disablement under practices capitalist projects, such as factory farming.

Animal farming is a practice of violence that causes multispecies disability—it is a "social injustice [than] can mark a body, steal a body, feed lies and poison to a body" (Clare, 2001, p. 362). Such practices have been understood through the ecoability paradigm, which recognizes the ways the animal and disability rights movements fight against normative conceptions of value and worth. Hog farming's relation to disability, both human and nonhuman, is a productive site for examining the impacts of the ecoability paradigm. Ecoability joins multiple social justice movements to recognize the ways in which animals and people with disabilities are impacted by normative conceptions of ability and competence and are often classified as sub-human (Nocella II et al., 2012a). Ecoability recognizes the shared concerns between animal advocacy, disability, and the environment, as well as the ways that these movements experience friction and sometimes work against each other, calling for a stronger coalition of liberatory movements.

As Dana Luciano and Mel Y. Chen explored in their introduction to their issue "Queer Inhumanisms" in *GLQ: A Journal of Lesbian and Gay Studies:*

> Many of queer theory's foundational texts interrogate, implicitly or explicitly, the nature of the 'human' in its relation to the queer, both in their attention to how sexual norms themselves constitute and regulate hierarchies of humanness, as they work to unsettle those norms and the default forms of humanness they uphold (Luciano & Chen, 2015, p. 186).

Factory farming is a "polluted politics," an ecopolitics that explores the impact of environmental degradation, including the effect of air and water pollution on what Giovanna Di Chiro calls the "body/home" (Erickson & Mortimer-Sandilands, 2010, p. 199–200). In addition to the mass murder of nonhuman life, those who live and work in close proximity to CAFOs, experience a slew of ailments. Further, the pollution literally seeps into the environment, disrupting entire ecosystems. Disability does not remain confined to the CAFO. Di Chiro argues that "bodies can be torn and stolen away," both the bodies of human and nonhuman animals, through polluted politics (Erickson & Mortimer-Sandilands, 2010, p.199).

Communities in eastern North Carolina are dealing with toxins, both literal and metaphorical. Following Mel Chen's description of a toxin as an invading figure, toxic pollution threatens and invades already stigmatized communities. These toxins bring with them disability to the local communities and CAFO workers, as well as nonhuman animal death, for the sake of capitalism. As Chen writes about toxins:

> A toxin threatens, but it also beckons. It is not necessarily alive, yet it enlivens morbidity and fear of death. A toxin requires an object against which it threat operates; this threatened object is an animal object—hence potentially also a kind of subject—whose "natural defenses" will be put to the test, in detection, in "fighting off," and finally in submission and absorption. (2011, p. 265)

Toxins disrupt and challenge the boundaries between life and death and queer our understandings of what it means to be in/human. Toxins have physical effects, and they are also implicated in "toxic constructs" and systems of oppression (Bentley, 2012). The theoretical tool of the toxin allows us to examine sociopolitical structures that are themselves toxic and damaging. Toxins also have real, material impacts on the environment of Duplin County, which creates disabled and disabling environments. This way of approaching disability shows that it is created through relational, multispecies encounters.

This understanding of toxicity and disability is inherently queer and queering. Hog farming can be seen as a "toxic chemical pollution responsible for the undermining or perversion of the 'natural'" (Erickson & Mortimer-Sandilands, 2010, p. 201). This destabilization of the normative troubles the culture/nature divide[5] and "challenge[s] the assumption that nature and the natural are neutral, independent categories" (Erickson & Mortimer-Sandilands, 2010, p. 232). As Katie Hogan has written:

> Queer critical interventions into such uses of nature and environment expose the dark purposes to which nature and environmentalism can be put. Disrupting, challenging, and undermining normative ideas of what counts as naturally fit and unfit is the primary emphasis (2010, p. 236).

This fit/unfit dualism is a construction integral to our institutions and cultural structures that prioritizes the lives and well-being of the normative body at the detriment of the nonnormative body, which is pathologized, restricted, and policed. This dualism supports capitalistic projects that lead to "toxic dumping in poor rural and urban areas," often POC communities (Erickson & Mortimer-Sandilands, 2010, p. 236). This toxic dumping effectively leads to the destruction of the bodies of these affected communities. This ableism is inherently a tool of violence institutionalized in our systems. Hog farming shows how multiple types of bodies are subjected to ableism and deemed less than able. This ableism contributes to further disability, as animals are maimed and murdered, workers experience injury and PTSD, and multispecies communities experience a host of other ailments. This is an example of what Taylor terms "disabled ecologies," which she describes as

> the webs of disability that are created spatially, temporally, and across species boundaries when ecosystems are contaminated, depleted, and profoundly altered. I understand disabled ecologies as the material and cultural ways disability is manifested and produced between and among human and nonhuman entities. (2019).

Disabled ecologies indicate the ways in which humans, often through projects of transnational capitalism, have altered the environment in ways that effectively limit its ability to function and foster sustainable multispecies communities. Disability is more than just a human condition; indeed, it is a more-than-human experience with wide-reaching consequences for addressing environmental harm and multispecies liberation.

Building on Chen's work, scholar Kelly Fritsch notes the similarities between discourses of toxins and disability: "Toxicity, like disability, is not contained in individually bounded bodies; it circulates, altering the life chances of future generations" (2017, p. 374). Toxins are deeply embedded in an environment that is not static, but laden with sociocultural political power. Thus, it is not enough to grapple with toxins on the scale of the individual body, to locate disability as an individualized problem, but to think relationally about multispecies relationships and disability.

As Eunjung Kim explains, "To think through disability from a critical inhumanist position is. . .to recalibrate our understanding of the human in a more accurate and inclusive" (2015, p. 305). Conditions of normalcy are rooted in raced, gendered, and classed ideals, and to strive for normalcy without questioning these may only serve to reinforce existing dynamics. Instead, we take a critical approach to queering the boundaries of what is considered the normative human. This fit/unfit dualism queers the toxic bodies and environment of Duplin County. The toxic body is the disrupting body—it has the capacity to destabilize hegemonic hierarchies of which bodies matter.

From this position, we call for ecological, multispecies help, without reinforcing the "ableist failure of imagination" (Kafer, 2013, p. 4) that reifies a return to a normative body as the only possible good future. Through ecoability, we can "desire disability differently" (Fritsch, 2015). This means seeing disability as a productive site for queering what it means to be human and what it means to be more-than-human. Disability, and ecoability, helps us imagine a more just world for all, one that works to dismantle connected oppressions around the boundaries of "normal" and "natural."

Queering Duplin County: The Potential for Disability Liberation

> [There is an] ongoing exposure of immigrants and people of color to risk that sets them up for condition of bodily work and residence that dramatize burdens that projects of white nationalism can hardly refuse to perceive (Chen, 2012, p. 173).

CAFO and slaughterhouse workers are often marginalized people of color (POC).[6] In 2007, only 33 % of these workers were U.S. citizens and 38 % of them did not speak English.[7] One out of two CAFO workers will be injured on the job by the five-year mark (Genoways, 2014). In 2012, the Center for Disease Control reported that there were around 20 deaths per every 100,000 CAFO workers (Patton, 2015). The poor air quality at CAFOs leads to respiratory issues in 70 % of their workers.[8] These workers also have high rates of PTSD linked to their jobs. Effectively, working in CAFOs is a disabling practice.

The communities surrounding the CAFOs in Duplin County are also majority low-income POC, both Black and Hispanic. CAFO workers consist primarily of the descendants of enslaved people, who have few other employment opportunities and a recent influx of Hispanic immigrants (Waltz, 2018). CAFOs are placed in these marginalized communities because these communities have less access to the sociopolitical capital necessary to combat CAFOs assault on their air, water, and bodies. The bodies of low-income POC are sacrificed to industrialized farming and the capitalist food regime. While these people may not consider themselves disabled or connect workplace injuries and chronic health problems with disability, their proximity to disability is informed by an ableist understanding of class and race.

Ableism positions certain groups of beings as more proximate to harm (Puar, 2017). While ableism is most simply understood as discrimination on the grounds of dis/ability, its effects are more wide-reaching. Ableism also informs which bodies are appropriate to be disabled, including POC, poor people, and nonhuman animals. One does not have to be disabled to experience ableism (Lewis, 2019). These ideals have devalued large groups of people and positioned them in ways that increase their likelihood of disablement through flows of toxins.

Animality has heavily figured into oppressions for those who are deemed less than the ideal white, male, capitalist citizen. The positioning of POC as animals has justified slavery, eugenics, and colonialism (Ko, 2017). These violences also make POC more likely to experience disability, in addition to being positioned as disabled. Disabled people have also been animalized (Taylor, 2017). Though experiences of disability are intertwined with experiences of race, there are connected experiences of being seen as unintelligent, freaks, and less valuable because of connections to animality. As many writers who contribute to the ecoability movement have elaborated open, the shared framings of animality and disability have been used to oppress various groups, including the nonhuman world (Nocella II et al., 2012b; Nocella II et al., 2017; Nocella II et al., 2019). These connections make the animal a powerful point of critique and multispecies liberation because it shows how animality is used to devalue certain bodies, both human and nonhuman.

While there is nothing inherently bad about being either an animal or being disabled, ableism, in combination with racism and speciesism, has positioned these ways of being as inferior. As Black vegan writer Syl Ko notes, when protesting against the animalization of Black and other POC, "there is an *open acceptance* of the negative status of 'the animal' [which] is a *tacit acceptance* of *the hierarchical racial system and white supremacy in general*" (2017, p. 45). In our attempts to fight injustice, we must avoid lateral oppression and recognize how ableism and eugenics informs views about what it means to be less-than-human, and the multiple forms of violence this has caused (Kim, 2015).

The Toxic Body as a Site of Resistance: The Potential for Multispecies Solidarity

Ecological disablement asks us to take a broad view of the systemic ways that disability is created and its more-than-human impacts. Hog farming has caused disability to spread through the ecosystem (Buford, November 23, 2018; Formuzis, July 11, 2016). Duplin County, considered a site of environmental racism, places POC, both literally and figuratively, close to animality and disability. As toxins flow through the landscape, they impact every aspect of the environment. This is a trans-corporeal effect that shows that bodies are not individual and bounded, neither are our movements for social justice. As a site of injustice, Duplin County shows interconnected violences, especially among those who are multiply marginalized.

While the effects of toxins are most pronounced in the impoverished, predominately Black and Hispanic communities of North Carolina's "Black Belt" region, they also travel through the landscape to impact communities farther downwind and downstream. We cannot argue against ableism without reckoning with the forms of violence that cause disproportionate harm to black and brown bodyminds; nor can we seek an end to factory farming without understanding the ways in which the category of "animal" has figured into the creation of the white, cisheteropatriarchal, settler-colonial state. While ableism has different impacts across groups, it has consistently served to devalue bodies. Connecting our understanding of ableism with ecoability shows that ableism also impacts the nonhuman environment.

In this chapter, we illustrated that there is a connection and shared oppression faced by factory farm workers, the animals produced for slaughter, and the local community and environment in Duplin County. In engaging with this case study through the frameworks of ecoability, ecological disablement, and queer ecologies, we were able to build a shared community including the non/human, creating what Donna Harraway has called "odd-kin" (2016, p. 4).

In conceptualizing the toxic body as an inherently queered space, we are able to imagine it as a site of resistance, connecting human communities affected by this toxicity to animals harmed in the mechanisms of violence, as well as the polluted environment. As Clare has explained, ". . .just as the body can be stolen, it can also be reclaimed. . .as a will to reconfigure the world" (Clare, 2001, p. 363). This reconfiguration depends on a multispecies solidarity and recognition that our world is filled with non/human entanglements (Tsing, 2015).

The nonhuman world and our own is inherently intertwined. We can imagine a futurity created by this multispecies solidarity that challenges the neoliberal capitalist system and dismantles the system of violence that harms human and nonhuman communities in its drive for profit (Fritsch, 2017). Recognizing these "entanglements" between the non/human creates an opportunity for us to challenge what is considered normative, connect, and integrate social movements that have historically been in their own separate silos, and subvert and dismantle the cisheteropatriarchal State that threatens, targets, and poisons nonhuman bodies, the environment, and marginalized human communities for the capitalist project.

Notes

1 https://www.ewg.org/interactive-maps/2017_NC_CAFO_PropertyRights.php
2 Quoted in *What the Health* https://observer.com/2017/05/pig-waste-factory-farming-north-carolina/
3 Quoted in https://www.ncbi.nlm.nih.gov/pmc/articles/PMC3672924/
4 This was brought down to 94 million because of a cap on damages. In 2017, Republican state lawmakers introduced a bill to limit damages sought by plaintiffs

affected by CAFOs, considered frivolous or " nuisance" lawsuits. This bill passed in the state legislature but was vetoed by North Carolina's governor, who noted that so-called nuisance lawsuits could be used to protect property rights, the environment, and make good changes. Despite the governor's stance, 2018 legislation tightened restrictions—plaintiffs must now live within a half mile of the farm and must file their lawsuit within a year of the CAFO beginning operation.

5 See Val Plumwood's Feminism *and the Mastery of Nature* (1993)
6 A total 72% are born outside the United States and 68% born in Mexico, according to the National Center for Farmworker Health, Inc.
7 2007–2009 National Agricultural Workers Survey (NAWS).
8 https://foodispower.org/factory-farm-workers/

References

Bentley, J. K. C. (2012). Human disabilities, nonhuman animals, and nature: Toxic constructs and transformative technologies. In A. J. Nocella II, J. K. C. Bentley, & J. M. Duncan (Eds.), *Earth, animal, and disability liberation: The rise of the eco-ability movement* (pp. 22–37). Peter Lang Publishing.

Buford, T. (2018, November 23). A hog waste agreement lacked teeth, and some North Carolinians say they're left to suffer. *ProPublica*. https://www.propublica.org/article/a-hog-waste-agreement-lacked-teeth-and-some-north-carolinians-say-left-to-suffer

Chen, M. Y. (2011). Toxic animacies, inanimate affections. *GLQ, 17*(2–3), 265–286.

Chen, M. Y. (2012). *Animacies: Biopolitics, racial mattering, and queer affect*. Durham, NC: Duke University Press.

Clare, E. (2001). Stolen bodies, reclaimed bodies: Disability and queerness. *Public Culture, 13*(3), 359–366.

Clark, D. B. (2018, March 19). Why is China treating North Carolina like the developing world? *Rolling Stone*. https://www.rollingstone.com/politics/politics-news/why-is-china-treating-north-carolina-like-the-developing-world-122892/

Duncan, C. (2019, February 8). Hurricane Florence was among the costliest disasters on record. *News & Observer*. https://www.newsobserver.com/news/state/north-carolina/article225974185.html

Erevelles N. (2014). Crippin' Jim Crow: Disability, dis-location, and the school-to-prison pipeline. In L. Ben-Moshe, C. Chapman, & A. C. Carey (Eds.), *Disability incarcerated* (pp. 81–99). Palgrave Macmillan.

Erickson, B., & Mortimer-Sandilands, C. (2010). *Queer ecologies: Sex, nature, politics, desire*. Bloomington, IN: Indiana University Press.

Formuzis, A. (2016, July 11). Manure in the Mist: Hog hell permeates Duplin County, N.C. *EWG*. https://www.ewg.org/agmag/2016/07/manure-mist-hog-hell-permeates-duplin-county-nc

Fritsch, K. (2015). Desiring disability differently: Neoliberalism, heterotopic imagination and intra-corporeal reconfigurations. *Foucault Studies, 19*, 43–66.

Fritsch, K. (2017). Toxic pregnancies: Speculative futures, disabling environments, and neoliberal biocapital. In S. J. Ray, & J. Sibara (Eds.), *Disability studies and the environmental humanities: Toward an eco-crip theory* (pp. 359–380). University of Nebraska Press.

Genoways, T. (2014, December 20). I felt like a piece of trash—Life inside Americas food processing plants. Retrieved from https://www.theguardian.com/world/2014/dec/21/life-inside-america-food-processing-plants-cheap-meat

Haraway, D. (2016). *Staying with the trouble: Making Kin in the Chthulucene*. Durham, NC: Duke University Press.

Hellerstein, E., & Fine, K. (2017, September 20). A million tons of feces and an unbearable stench: Life near industrial pig farms. *The Guardian*.

Human Rights Watch. (2005). *Blood, sweat, and fear: Workers' rights in U.S. meat and poultry plants*. https://www.hrw.org/sites/default/files/reports/usa0105.pdf

Human Rights Watch. (2019). *"When we're dead and buried, our bones will keep hurting:" Workers' rights under threat in US meat and poultry plants*. https://www.hrw.org/sites/default/files/report_pdf/us0919_web.pdf

Kafer, A. (2013). *Feminist queer crip*. Indiana University Press.

Kim, E. (2015). Unbecoming human: An ethics of objects. *GLQ: A Journal of Lesbian and Gay Studies, 21*(2–3), 295–320.

Ko, S. (2017). Addressing racism requires addressing the situation of animals. In A. Ko & S. Ko (Eds.), *Aphro-ism: Essays on pop culture, feminism, and black veganism from two sisters* (pp. 44–49). Lantern Books.

Kravchenko, J., Rhew, S. H., Akushevich, I., Agarwal, P., & Lyerly, H. K. (2018). Mortality and health outcomes in North Carolina communities located in close proximity to hog concentrated animal feeding operations. *North Carolina Medical Journal, 79*(5), 278–288.

Kuo, L. (2015, July 14). The world eats cheap bacon at the expense of North Carolina's rural poor. *Quartz*. https://qz.com/433750/the-world-eats-cheap-bacon-at-the-expense-of-north-carolinas-rural-poor/

Leibler, J. H., Janulewicz, P. A., & Perry M. J. (2017). Prevalence of serious psychological distress among slaughterhouse workers at a United States beef packing plant. *Work, 57*(1), 105–109. https://doi.org/10.3233/WOR-172543

Lewis, T. L. (2019). *Longmore Lecture: Context, Clarity, and Grounding.* Tu[r]ning into self. https://www.talilalewis.com/blog/longmore-lecture-context-clarity-grounding

Luciano, D., & Chen, M. Y. (2015). Has the Queer Ever Been Human? *GLQ: A Journal of Lesbian and Gay Studies, 21*(2–3), 183–207.

Lupinacci, J., & Lupinacci, M. W. (2017). (Re)Imaginings of 'Community:' Perceptions of (ids)ability, the environment, and inclusion." In A. J. Nocella II, A. E. George, & J. L. Schatz (Eds.), *The intersectionality of critical animal, disability, and environmental studies: Toward eco-ability, justice, and liberation* (pp. 63–78). Lexington Books.

Marks, R. (2001). Cesspools of shame: How factory farms lagoons and sprayfields threaten environmental and public health. *Natural Resources Defense Council.* https://www.nrdc.org/sites/default/files/cesspools.pdf

Murawski, J. (2018, October 24). The amount of E. coli and fecal matter in NC wells has spiked since Hurricane Florence. *News & Observer.* https://amp.newsobserver.com/news/business/article220561095.html

Nicole W. (2013). CAFOs and environmental justice: The case of North Carolina. *Environmental Health Perspectives, 121*(6), A182–A189. https://doi.org/10.1289/ehp.121-a182

Nocella II, A. J., Bentley, J. K. C., & Duncan, J. M. (2012a). Introduction: The rise of eco-ability. In A. J. Nocella II, J. K. C. Bentley, & J. M. Duncan (Eds.), *Earth, animal, and disability liberation: The rise of the eco-ability movement* (pp. xiii-xxii). Peter Lang Publishing.

Nocella II, A. J., Bentley, J. K. C., & Duncan, J. M. (Eds.). (2012b). *Earth, animal, and disability liberation: The rise of the eco-ability movement.* Peter Lang Publishing.

Nocella II, A. J., George, A. E., & Lupinacci, J. (Eds.). (2019). *Animals, disability, and the end of capitalism: Voices from the eco-ability movement.* Peter Lang Publishing.

Nocella II, A. J., George, A. E., & Schatz, J. L. (Eds.). (2017). *The intersectionality of critical animal, disability, and environmental studies: Toward eco-ability, justice, and liberation.* Lexington Books.

Patton, L. (2015). The human victims of factory farming. Retrieved from https://www.onegreenplanet.org/environment/the-human-victims-of-factory-farming/

Pierre-Louis, K. (2018, September 19). Lagoons of pig waste are overflowing after Florence. *New York Times.* https://www.nytimes.com/2018/09/19/climate/florence-hog-farms.html

Puar, J. K. (2017). *The right to maim: Debility, capacity, disability.* Duke University Press.

Schiffman, S. S., Sattely Miller, E. A., Suggs, M. S., & Graham, B. G. (1995). The effect of environmental odors emanating from commercial swine operations on the mood of nearby residents. *Brain Research Bulletin, 37*(4), 369–375.

Sorg, L. (2020, January 24). Environmental groups, scientists say DEQs air monitoring program fails the sniff test. Retrieved from http://www.ncpolicywatch.com/2020/01/24/environmental-groups-scientists-say-deqs-air-monitoring-program-fails-the-sniff-test/

Sturgis, S. (2017, April 19). Mapping those affected by North Carolina's factory-farm protection bill. *Facing South.* https://www.facingsouth.org/2017/04/mapping-those-affected-north-carolinas-factory-farm-protection-bill

Taylor, S. (2017). *Beasts of burden: Animal and disability liberation.* The New Press.

Taylor, S. (2019). Disabled ecologies: Living with impaired landscapes. Lecture at UC Berkeley, March 5. https://haasinstitute.berkeley.edu/video-sunaura-taylor-disabled-ecologies-living-impaired-landscapes

Tsing, A. L. (2015). *The mushroom at the end of the world.* Princeton University Press.

Waltz, L. (2018). *Hog wild: The battle for workers' rights at the world's largest slaughterhouse*. University of Iowa Press.

Wing, S., & Johnston, J. (2014, August 29). Industrial hog operations in North Carolina disproportionately impact African-Americans, Hispanics, and American Indians. *NC Policy Watch*. http://www.ncpolicywatch.com/wp-content/uploads/2014/09/UNC-Report.pdf

Yeoman, B. (2019, August 27). 'It smells like a decomposing body': North Carolina's polluting pig farms. *The Guardian*. https://www.theguardian.com/environment/2019/aug/27/it-smells-like-a-decomposing-body-north-carolinas-polluting-pig-farms

Yeoman, B. (2019, December 20). Here are the rural residents who sued the world's largest hog producer over waste and odors—and won. Retrieved from https://thefern.org/2019/12/rural-north-carolinians-won-multimillion-dollar-judgments-against-the-worlds-largest-hog-producer-will-those-cases-now-be-overturned/

5. Trauma-Informed Activism: New Directions for Interspecies Trauma in Ecoability and Critical Animal Studies

T.N. ROWAN

Content warning: This chapter includes descriptions of trauma and violence against nonhuman animals. Due to my own ethical positioning and interest in trauma and disability the content warnings in this chapter are usually subtle and indicated by *italics*. I have purposely not included any graphic or extremely detailed descriptions.

Introduction

A vegan lifestyle typically involves learning about and mentally processing significant amounts of violence. Donald Watson and five others first used the term "vegan" in 1944 and established The Vegan Society of England; however, abstaining from eating and using nonhuman animals has been practiced by people of many cultures for thousands of years (The Vegan Society, n.d.). Watson once said: "One of our critics informs us that the reform we advocate is 'so very difficult.' *The cow too must not find it easy when her successive calves are taken away from her, but she can do nothing about it. We can*" (as cited in Cole, 2014, p. 209). Cows and other animals have more agency than often given credit for, but Watson is correct to imply that humans have a privileged position when it comes to interspecies encounters. If given a choice many people would probably agree it is easier and preferable to eat plants than to endure the violence humans force upon cows. It is a privilege that in the West the majority of humans never have to witness or think about the animal violence they benefit from and financially support. Many texts have already been written about the importance of veganism for acting in solidarity with nonhuman animals and marginalized human groups (Harper, 2010; Nocella II et al., 2014; Sorenson, 2014). Future intersectional writing on this topic continues to be important. In this chapter I use an Ecoability framework to discuss trauma as one of the difficult parts of going vegan, not to disrupt the vegan movement, but rather to support its future flourishing.

In the 1990s researchers publicly recognized that health care staff such as therapists and nurses can develop compassion fatigue, vicarious trauma, and secondary stress from hearing about the violence their patients have endured (Nimmo & Huggard, 2013, pp. 37–8; Way et al., 2004, p. 49). On blog posts, *YouTube* videos, and podcasts there is a growing but overall small concern about how witnessing violence against nonhuman animals affects vegans through burn out, secondary traumatic stress, or Secondary-Traumatic Stress Disorder (STSD). The symptoms of STSD mimic Post-Traumatic Stress Disorder (PTSD), but STSD affects individuals who see or hear about violence rather than directly experience it (Callie & Nichole, 2016; Joy, 2015). As J. Ang writes in a blog post for *In Defense of Animals*:

> If you're vegan or thinking about going vegan, chances are pretty high that you've been exposed to some very disturbing information—whether it was in the form of a written article, a video, or a story told by a friend. The level of violence involved in the meat, dairy, egg, and other industries that use animals can be quite extreme, and it's only natural if you've felt upset or even traumatized by it. (2016, para. 3)

Learning about veganism often includes processing significant amounts of violence. Echoing Ang's concern, C. L. Wrenn asserts that "the violence we witness causes real psychological damage. While I think it is important that we have a knowledge about the institutions of speciesism, I question whether or not repeated exposure to this violence is healthy" (2014, para. 3). Vegans can also develop STSD even if they have never personally witnessed violence against nonhuman animals or seen violent videos or images; *believing that nonhuman animals are sentient and then seeing the after-effects of their being killed or used repeatedly in everyday life as "food" or "clothing" can be traumatizing* (Callie & Nichole, 2016).

Some scholars have suggested that vicarious trauma in health care workers is a "normal consequence of working in a caring and helping profession" and that it is important to depathologize and normalize vicarious trauma (Nimmo & Huggard, 2013, p. 37). These goals are in line with how Ecoability as a field affirms that "all people are different and have unique needs" and challenges the perception that people with disabilities need to be fixed (Nocella

II, 2012, p. 17). This chapter strikes a careful balance when unpacking STSD within the vegan community by beginning with a discussion of what trauma is and critiques of the medical model of STSD. Second, I explain how STSD does the important theoretical work of taking nonhuman animals seriously while also opening up questions about normalized activist practices. I discuss how some suggestions intended to support vegans living with STSD come from good intentions but problematize the individual. I conclude by developing a theory of Trauma-Informed Activism that draws on Trauma-Informed Care literature, Trauma-Informed Meditation and Yoga literature, and my experiences as a scholar and activist (Forner, 2017). The chapter includes practical suggestions for how the vegan community, Ecoability, and Critical Animal Studies (CAS) can shift to include vegans with STSD (Nocella II, Bentley, & Duncan, 2012; Nocella II, Sorenson, Socha, & Matsuoko, 2014).

Defining Trauma and STSD

C. Caruth defines trauma as *"the response to an unexpected or overwhelming violent event or events that are not fully grasped as they occur, but return later in repeated flashbacks, nightmares, and other repetitive phenomena"* (1996, p. 91). J. Herman explains trauma is a subjective response because "no two people have identical reactions, even to the same event," and everyone expresses symptoms or features of trauma differently (2015, p. 58). Trauma responses range from "a brief stress reaction that gets better by itself and never qualifies for a diagnosis, to classic or simple post-traumatic stress disorder, to the complex syndrome of prolonged, repeated trauma" (p. 119). For Herman the core experiences of trauma are feelings of *"disempowerment and disconnection from others"* (p. 133). L. van Dernoot Lipsky and C. Burk identify the following 16 warning signs of trauma exposure response in social justice activists: *feeling helpless and hopeless, a sense of never doing enough, hypervigilance, diminished creativity, inability to embrace complexity, minimizing, chronic exhaustion/physical ailments, inability to listen/deliberate avoidance, dissociative moments, sense of persecution, guilt, fear, anger and cynicism, inability to empathize/numbing, addictions, and grandiosity* (2009, pp. 47–113). Other potential symptoms of trauma specifically noticed in vegans include: *chronic worry and anxiety, intrusive thoughts, increased irritability, nightmares, flashbacks, difficulty concentrating, panic attacks, becoming withdrawn, viewing the world through a hostile lens/loss of faith in humanity, depression, and appetite changes* (Ang, 2016; Joy, 2015; Mann, 2014; Taft, 2016). These affective shifts and experiences are understandable reactions to witnessing violence that a person cannot make sense of or come to terms with

(Herman, 2015, p. 51). Instead of being processed, the violence is held inside a person's bodymind and reverberates outward again and again as an affective shift in repetitive, belated, incomprehensive, and intrusive ways (Caruth, 1996, p. 92; Carter, 2015, para. 5). Vegans could have trauma from their own life events and/or have trauma from witnessing or hearing about violence against nonhuman animals.

A significant reverberation of trauma occurs when a person is triggered. As A. M. Carter describes:

> To be triggered is to mentally and physically re-experience a past trauma in such an embodied manner that one's affective response literally takes over the ability to be present in one's bodymind. When this occurs, the triggered individuals often feel a complete loss of control and disassociation from the bodymind. This is not a state of injury, but rather a state of disability. (2015, para. 7)

This state of disability changes over time and is not necessarily permanent. Following Nocella II and other scholars and activists I use disabled and disability as reclaimed terms and recognize they refer to an "identifiable group that needs assistance and is challenged in the current exclusionary society in which we live" (2012, pp. 16–17). Being triggered involves encountering a disabling reminder of the original traumatic event(s), although this reminder may not always be consciously identified (Lockhart, 2016). For many, part of learning to live with and process trauma includes learning to identify your triggers. *Triggers vary considerably and may be a direct reminder of the event, such as being in the same geographic location, or hearing about a similar event, such as reading about sexual assault statistics after being sexually assaulted.* Even learning about triggers themselves or reading about trauma can be triggering. Notice that a significant amount of this section on defining trauma and STSD has been italicized for content warnings. For vegans specifically the world itself can become traumatizing and *seeing the bodies of nonhuman animals at the grocery store or on someone else's plate can be triggering* (Callie & Nichole, 2016). *The difficulties of living with trauma can be exacerbated when vegans are routinely warned by vegans and nonvegans not to object to seeing humans eat animal products lest they become the "angry vegan" that no one wants to listen to or take seriously. Triggered reactions are sometimes dismissed as being "too emotional" or damaging to the vegan movement because they alienate nonvegans.* While it is important to be supportive and encouraging to nonvegans, it is also important to validate and support the understandable reactions vegans have to witnessing and remembering violence.

In this chapter trauma and STSD are often interwoven, but the medical diagnosis of having a disorder is complex. Some individuals benefit from being diagnosed because it gives them greater access to accommodations and can provide them with a theoretical framework to understand what they are going through. For example, early treatment of PTSD can include helping people identify their symptoms and understand that they are not abnormal or a sign of weakness (Härle, 2017, pp. 67–68). Relying on a diagnosis as proof of trauma can be problematic because diagnoses are not equally accessible to all people, people can be misdiagnosed, individuals may struggle to explain their symptoms in ways that match up with a diagnosis, and some people may not feel comfortable or safe entering the medical system. At the time of writing this chapter, PTSD is included in the American Psychiatric Association's most recent Diagnostic and Statistical Manual of Mental Disorders, the DSM-5. The DSM-5 hints at Complex Post-Traumatic Stress Disorder (C-PTSD) but does not include it (Phillips, 2015; Herman, 2015, p. 257). It does not include STSD. The 11th edition of the International Classification of Diseases from the World Health Organization includes PTSD and C-PTSD as separate "sibling" disorders (Hyland et al., 2018). C-PTSD is unique in that it refers to trauma from prolonged and repeated exposure to events, especially during childhood (Herman, 2015, pp. 119, 257). Individuals in North America who have trauma from prolonged and repeated exposure may not be diagnosed as having trauma. The lack of recognition of C-PTSD is especially problematic because *many victims of abuse often minimize their trauma or have it minimized by others because it "wasn't that bad."* C-PTSD is significant for vegans, because while many vegans may develop trauma from witnessing a single violent event, vegans can also develop trauma from viewing hundreds of images and videos of violence against nonhuman animals over a period of months or years. This second example would be harder for the vegan to identify and thus deserves further attention.

Lastly, I frame trauma in this chapter as interspecies, meaning that I am interested in trauma that occurs among or between species. Vegans with STSD develop their trauma as a result of witnessing violence against nonhuman animals. *Some humans, particularly those belonging to marginalized populations, develop trauma from working in slaughterhouses and other places where animals are used* (LaCapra, 2016, p. 398; Nibert, 2014). Nonhuman animals themselves can also develop trauma across species boundaries. *Nonhuman animals are problematically given PTSD to be used as medical models for human PTSD* (Diamond et al., 2012; Ebenezer et al., 2016; Stam, 2007), which indicates that other animals experience trauma that is comparable to how humans experience it. *Notably the trauma is considered comparable enough that nonhuman animals can serve as a medical model to benefit humans, but not close enough to make it ethically or legally suspect to give nonhuman animals trauma on purpose.* This flawed logic is not an exception limited to the medical industry, but representative of how nonhuman animals are treated on a vast scale. As G. Bradshaw explains:

> *Domesticated animals experience their own brand of relational trauma. Babies are torn from their families, forced to live under horrendous conditions, and in the case of farmed and other commodified animals such as greyhounds, eventually killed. Even in the case of "companion" animals such as cats and dogs, kittens and puppies are prematurely stolen from their parents, their natural social and emotional processes are ignored. From the perspective of attachment theory—the science of how minds and emotions are shaped through early relationships—"breeding" and "husbandry" practices comprise violent relational trauma.* (Goodman & Bradshaw, 2015, p. 1)

Human interaction with other species regularly involves systemic oppression that nonhuman animals may experience as PTSD, C-PTSD, and trauma. D. LaCapra (2016) has written about including CAS' ethical work on nonhuman animals into interdisciplinary research on identity, history, trauma, and memory. Future work in these directions is especially important.

The Theoretical Work of STSD

Writing about and discussing vegans with STSD is significant because it simultaneously represents nonhuman animals as subjects of violence. *Domesticating, confining, breeding, separating from their friends or family members, and killing nonhuman animals* are considered to be legal, normal, and ethically acceptable. STSD challenges this framework by claiming that vegans are traumatized by witnessing violence against nonhuman animals. Thus, what nonhuman animals endure is automatically represented and respected as violence. Discussing the challenges vegans with STSD face does not minimize or reject the violence nonhuman animals face, but rather affirms and validates that violence. Vegans with STSD theoretically say to nonhuman animals: "What you have endured is something so violent that I cannot even process it. It is a violence that cannot be contained by my body-mind and I feel it so deeply that it reverberates through me, over and over again." I believe discussing STSD includes humans acting in solidarity with nonhuman animals and using their own trauma to bring greater recognition to the systematic violence that nonhuman animals endure.

Scholars and activists who discuss vegans with STSD often suggest that these people should turn to fellow vegans or the vegan community for support and limit intake of violent content. Many people have personally shared to activist and psychologist M. Joy that they are traumatized from watching

Earthlings for the fourth time or so. Both Joy and Wrenn suspect that some vegans repeatedly watch violent content showing nonhuman animal suffering because of their own internal guilt (Joy, 2015; Wrenn, 2014). Wrenn also argues some vegans may repeatedly watch violent content to prove that they are strong enough to do so, in the process further entrenching androcentrism in the vegan movement that problematically disparages "female 'emotionality' and the embracing of violent-tolerant masculinity" (2014, para. 10). As already discussed, guilt, minimizing one's own hardship, numbing, and a sense of never doing enough are all warning signals of potential trauma and STSD. In other words, vegans could be engaging in repeatedly watching violent content because they are already traumatized and do not have the awareness, tools, or support to respond to their own trauma in other ways. Ang encourages individuals struggling to join "a vegan community or meet-up group to share your experiences in a supportive environment," watch videos and read books created to support vegans, reach out to like-minded people, and "limit or eliminate your exposure to graphic animal cruelty scenes if you can" (2016, paras. 23–24). Ang also shares an important resource of the Activist Mentor Line phone number and email (2016, para. 24). Similarly, Joy suggests getting support from friends, family, colleagues, and a therapist and to "witness carefully" (2015). These suggestions are helpful, but they ignore that violent texts are regularly produced by and circulate in the vegan community and CAS.

STSD brings greater attention to the violence nonhuman animals endure, but also opens up questions about normalized activist practices. One of the most popular forms of activism is showing video footage or pictures of nonhuman animals being killed or suffering. It is common to include these pictures in the middle of a pamphlet about veganism that appears nonthreatening or to set up television screens or hold up computers in public places like subways and on the street. Vegan communities on websites like *Facebook* and *Reddit* contain similar content when vegans share advertisements to activist events, express their frustration at witnessing violence, and want to inform others. Academic articles in CAS, Ecoability, and other fields often contain detailed descriptions of violence against nonhuman animals to educate the reader and support important claims. I share no citations or references because I do not want to single out a specific individual or group as responsible, but I believe these examples will resonate with people who belong to or have spent time in these communities. In my activist work in vegan communities for over ten years, and reading CAS texts for around seven years, I have noticed that this practice is widespread, normal, and rarely questioned. I have also participated in this kind of activism myself because I once thought "that's just how it is done." Being a scholar and/or activist requires engagement with these texts because there is arguably no way to escape them and remain in these communities. Importantly the practice of sharing violent content to educate, bear witness, and force others to come to terms with the obscured violence around them is an act of solidarity with nonhuman animals and is done with the best of intentions. My own intention is not to shame or discredit activists and scholars who use these practices, but to suggest that theorizing about STSD is a way to ask critical and important questions about disability and intersectionality.

The majority of suggestions for vegans with STSD focus on the individual and what they can do to help themselves or garner support from others, but this makes the individual seem like the problem. The individual with STSD is typically expected to ask for accommodations, support, or things to be different. How each vegan community responds to this problem differs, but importantly the burden is placed on the vegan with STSD to disclose, explain, and defend their disability. Vegans can also start their own support or activist communities, but may find it difficult to find others to join them and to educate vegans who do not understand their need to limit violent content. Leading comes with its own challenges, and I have personally struggled with feelings of guilt and worrying that I was selfish for developing small vegan communities that are accessible to me. However, as Ecoability affirms, if external environmental factors make people disabled, vegans with STSD are truly enriching the vegan community by requesting that their differing abilities be embraced. People have disabilities not because they are abnormal or something needs to be fixed about them, but because society has failed to include the differing abilities of a particular group (Nocella II et al., 2012a, p. xiii). For example, in the West I am not disabled for being near-sighted because society is set up in such a way that people of my economic class can easily access glasses. Western society and most vegan and CAS spaces do not expect or account for vegans with STSD, or people with STSD, PTSD, C-PTSD, or undiagnosed trauma, and thus their differing abilities can be experienced as disability. Vegan communities and CAS can grow to create better access for vegans with STSD and anyone living with trauma. The burden of advocating for and defending these changes should not fall on disabled individuals.

Trauma-Informed Activism

Vegan communities and CAS would benefit from assuming that community members currently live with or may develop trauma in the future.

Acknowledging this reality requires organizational shifts that I propose be referred to as Trauma-Informed Activism. The term "Trauma-Informed Activism" has been used by a few activists, but there is limited data available about it online. In February 2020 The Canadian Community Economic Development Network hosted an event "Healing for Change: Trauma-Informed Activism" that explored "what it means to 'be the change we want to see in the world' by connecting theories of social changes with our own experience of oppression, privilege, trauma, empowerment, and freedom" (The Canadian CED Network, 2020). In March 2016, March 2017, and November 2018 Students Against Sexual Assault from Smith College held Trauma-Informed Activism workshops at their college (Students Against Sexual Assault 2016, 2017, 2018). I have not found attempts to define, identify, or advocate for Trauma-Informed Activism on a wider level. From this information I suggest that the proposal for Trauma-Informed Activism in this chapter is not necessarily new because it references ideas that other activists are already thinking about and perhaps have discussed using other terms. However, what is new is linking Trauma-Informed Activism to STSD and Ecoability, and advocating for shifts in community cultures in veganism, CAS, and other activist and scholarly groups.

My use of the term "Trauma-Informed Activism" is influenced by Trauma-Informed Care, which gained federal attention in the United States in the late 1990s and has been the topic of a significant amount of research, literature, and programs (Chaudhri et al., 2019; DeCandia & Guarino, 2015, p. 13; Muskett, 2014). This chapter does not provide a complete overview of Trauma-Informed Care or other related practices, but rather explains them generally to draw out theoretical and practical ideas that can be of use to activism. Trauma-Informed Care at minimum involves endeavoring "to do no further harm and avoid retraumatizing clients" (DeCandia & Guarino, 2015, p. 14; Muskett, 2014, p. 58). Traditional service systems assume that service providers are experts and that clients must be compliant. *Force, coercion, locking doors, seclusion, rigid rules, and lack of confidentiality* "often leave trauma survivors feeling abused by the system and reluctant to trust service providers" (DeCandia & Guarino, 2015, p. 15; Muskett, 2014, p. 58). Trauma-Informed Care focuses on "trauma knowledge, safety, choice, empowerment, and cultural competence" to build employees' knowledge, awareness, and skills to support the recovery of individuals (DeCandia & Guarino, 2015, p. 14). In the case of Trauma-Informed Activism the employees would be community leaders and members. Their goal would not be to help individuals recover (a framework Ecoability would challenge), but rather to empower and support individuals by using trauma knowledge to foster accessibility, safety, and choice.

Trauma-Informed or Trauma-Sensitive Meditation and Yoga developed out of Trauma-Informed Care to better accommodate practitioners with trauma. As S. Schlote explains, "mindfulness meditation and yoga are often suggested to clients with trauma to support their healing, without an understanding of the caveats and contradictions" (2015, p. 4). Both practices can be triggering and retraumatizing by exacerbating or further entrenching traumatic symptoms (Schlote, 2015; Treleaven, 2018, p. xxiv). For example, without the right guidance meditation can become a "cerebral and dissociative practice" for anyone (Treleaven, 2018, p. xxii), but this is particularly problematic for people living with trauma who turn to meditation to learn to stop or manage dissociating. People may dissociate during meditation or yoga by "thinking about their bodies instead of practicing inside them" (Treleaven, 2018, p. 127). Meditating and dissociation are both altered states of awareness and consciousness, but they are distinctly different as C. C. Forner explains: "Dissociation is often the deficiency of internal and external awareness; mindfulness is internal and external awareness in abundance. One is a brain function that is designed to know; the other is a brain function that is designed to not know" (2017, p. 11). *People may dissociate from their bodies and pull away from their own inner worlds to "cut off from the warning signals that they're constantly being bombarded with. This helps survivors manage traumatic symptoms," but when they are asked to notice their inner world through meditation or yoga it can be intense, frightening, and confusing* (Treleaven, 2015, p. 127). Meditation teachers who do not understand trauma will also not be able to recognize that their students are dissociating and may unintentionally invalidate and dis-empower them. These same issues can occur in yoga. Trauma-Informed Yoga teachers are taught to expect that dissociation, hypervigilance, hyperarousal, and memories, fears, or pains associated with the original trauma(s) may come into the classroom (Härle, 2017, p. 100). D. A. Treleaven argues, "It's our responsibility to adapt mindfulness to meet the specific needs of trauma survivors as opposed to expecting them to adapt to us" (2018, p. xxii).

So what does adapting our communities and practices to meet the needs of trauma survivors actually look like? There are countless ways to answer this question, and no one set of answers will be complete or work for everyone. As noted, trauma functions differently for different people. The remainder of this chapter includes possible practical suggestions to try and theoretical considerations to ponder. First, I propose that well-researched and ongoing education about trauma and STSD have an important place in the vegan community and CAS. In Trauma-Informed Care practices staff are provided with regular training on trauma and its impact and "the impact that working with trauma survivors has on providers (e.g., secondary traumatic stress)" (DeCandia & Guarino, 2015, p. 15). This training could be an integral part of activist workshops or shared and discussed regularly at activist meetings and planning sessions. As part of Trauma-Sensitive Meditation Treleaven advocates for continued partnership between mindfulness practitioners and trauma professionals (2018, p. xxiv). Our communities have much to learn from our own members and people outside of them who regularly research and write about trauma. Melanie Joy and Clare Mann are both vegan psychologists with much to say on the links between trauma and vegan activism. By consistently sharing information about trauma and STSD community members will be supported in identifying if and how trauma has affected them (Joy, 2015; van Dernoot Lipsky & Burk, 2009, p. 3). This information should also include practices that support a culture of self-care (DeCandia & Guarino, 2015, p. 15). From this knowledge and reflection activists can do the important work of committing to taking care of their needs, which should be done in a preventative and daily way. Getting enough sleep and eating regularly are both things activists may know about but continue to forget or place little priority on (Ang, 2016; Joy, 2015). Daily self-care can also include 30 minutes of unstructured time to do nothing, a gratitude practice, yoga, meditation, journaling, and exercise (Härle, 2017, p. 109; Joy, 2015; Mann, 2014). Activists can also cultivate their self-awareness and make note of their thoughts, triggers, and what makes them upset in a broader context of how they can learn and grow from these experiences (Joy, 2015; van Dernoot Lipsky & Burk, 2009, p. 6).

The second way that vegan and CAS communities can include vegans with STSD is by recognizing trauma as political. Trauma is not an individualized medical illness, but rather part of "a larger framework of systematic oppression and liberation theory" (van Dernoot Lipsky & Burk, 2009, p. 28; Treleaven, 2018, p. xxiv). Trauma is influenced by environmental factors and, at least partly, socially determined (DeCandia & Guarino, 2015, p. 12). As van Dernoot Lipsky and Burk explain: "Oppression plays a leading role in creating and maintaining systems that perpetuate suffering and trauma for all sentient beings, as well as the planet we share" (2009, p. 28). Physical violence, harassment, intimidation, and micro-aggressions may all lead to trauma in marginalized people. It is especially significant to have an ongoing commitment to "increasing one's consciousness about the ways people are impacted by systems of oppression, including how this relates to trauma," if a person has been "more sheltered from oppression and experienc[ed] more privilege" (Treleaven, 2018, pp. 147, 149). As Carter explains, whether we consider the effects of trauma "is a choice only for those whose lives are not already shaped by trauma. For us, there is no choice; our experiences of trauma shape how we move through the world" (2015, para. 1). Deciding not to think about trauma and not noticing that trauma affects others are both privileges and thus political concerns. Some Trauma-Informed practices share Disability Studies' goal of political advocacy and challenge the juxtaposition of disability with ability because the latter is relative, temporary, and not a norm (Berger, 2004, pp. 570, 577). Notably, Trauma Studies and Disability Studies have limited overlap in references, and trauma is sometimes considered to be a symptom rather than disabling (Berger, 2004, p. 563). Thus, thinking about trauma in a political framework can be an important link between Disability Studies and Trauma Studies and other fields that regularly focus on the politics of intersectional oppression like Ecoability, CAS, Environmental Studies, and feminism.

Third, vegan and CAS communities can better accommodate vegans with STSD by making choice a normal part of activist culture. As Härle explains in terms of Trauma-Sensitive Yoga:

> *In significantly traumatic situations, trauma clients experience a loss of control. We therefore provide them with a maximum of control.* We encourage them to see our recommendations and advice as offers, examine the interventions in terms of their success, and reject or modify interventions that are not very helpful. (2017, pp. 115–116)

Providing choice or options helps people living with trauma feel in control of their own lives and empowered. It is important to "leave people in choice" by never forcing, letting people move at a pace that works for them, and encouraging people to opt out, leave, or take a break if it is right for them (Treleaven, 2018, pp. 136–137). While these recommendations are made for yoga and meditation classes, they are also relevant to activist meetings, protests, workshops, planning sessions, or other activities. Providing endless choices is not helpful either though. Too many variations could be perceived as overwhelming, and some people living with trauma may have little bodymind awareness and struggle to make choices. Thus, a careful balance between not only offering choice but also requesting feedback on how much structure and freedom would be best for everyone is a good middle ground (Härle, 2017, p. 150). Every group or individual will be different, and the same group may have different needs on different days.

Providing choice requires that someone is structuring the process, which I suggest be done through a facilitator role. The facilitator is responsible for ensuring, as best they can, that everyone feels safe, included, and able to participate. The facilitator can openly discuss with all participants what ground rules would make everyone feel comfortable. Van Dernoot Lipsky and Burk encourage developing a chosen group into a microculture that showers members with encouragement and holds them accountable. "Its members must be people we can debrief with, laugh with, brainstorm with, consult with, cry with, and become better people with" (2009, p. 185). Notably this process does not spontaneously occur and must be guided and nourished. Other suggestions facilitators may want to keep in mind in Trauma-Informed spaces include: offering a predictable schedule, clearly marking the exits, having gender-neutral bathrooms, and keeping the room well-lit (Härle, 2017, p. 119; Treleaven, 2018, pp. 146–147). Lastly, if possible there should be more than one facilitator, and activists should take time sharing the facilitator role so that no person is expected to be "on" all the time.

Students Against Sexual Assault suggest Trauma-Informed Activism includes "giving individuals choice in how to participate in campaigns and activities" (2018). Choice can be incorporated into vegan activist and CAS communities by supporting a variety of content and events. For example, some activists get together after emotionally draining protests to socialize, unwind, and support each other. Members who have to stop attending events because they experience trauma or could never attend those events to begin with miss out on a significant amount of social support. An alternative could be organizing social events that do not make emotionally draining activism the anchor that bonds everyone together. While these other social events already exist, they are rarely Trauma-Informed and some activists look down on them because they are not "real activism." Furthermore, they often have limited attendance because some activists feel that making friends and support structures is not as important as directly protesting nonhuman animal use. It is important to challenge ideas about what activism should look like and the unrealistic goal of meeting this standard regardless of the personal or community cost. As discussed previously, carrying guilt, shame, or feelings of not doing or being enough are all early warning signs of STSD.

Trauma-Informed Care includes "reducing potentially triggering or retraumatizing practices" (DeCandia & Guarino, 2015, p. 15). This reduction is possible in vegan activism by widening our scope of activism itself. A list of possible events that may be more accessible to people with trauma include: social events where one ground rule is that violence against nonhuman animals will not be discussed at that particular event, coffee shop or tea meetups, doing yoga together with fellow vegans in a local park, making a zine together, writing political fiction, having a de-stress coloring hangout, volunteering at an animal sanctuary, hosting a fundraiser for an animal sanctuary, organizing a nutrition workshop, drawing pro-vegan comics or other art to put online, making a list of easy vegan recipes, designing a vegan grocery shopping list, networking with other political groups that are not already vegan, writing positive reviews for local vegan restaurants, and emailing businesses and asking them to carry more vegan options. While it is important to do activism that educates nonvegans about veganism, it is also significant to do activism that makes it easier for people to go and stay vegan. Explaining how to live as a vegan, rather than debating or defending veganism, was actually the first focus of The Vegan Society in England (Cole, 2014, p. 206). Vegan activism can also include developing empowering relationships with nonhuman animals and facilitating their agency. Some suggestions include: letting nonhuman animals decide if or how they will interact with humans, supporting animals living with their chosen family or friends, reducing or removing the use of restraints, and prioritizing bonding activities that the animals like to do. A rescued mule I used to work with especially loved going for walks in the forest with me.

Choice also includes the ability to opt out before being triggered or re-traumatized, which makes verbal and written content warnings a critical part of vegan activist and CAS communities. Joy encourages vegans to support each other by not making people "unintentional witnesses." "Ask people before you tell them horrible stories so that they don't get traumatized by over-witnessing" (Joy, 2015). For example, in vegan groups on social media platforms like *Facebook* put potentially triggering content under a "read more" and provide a content warning. In academic articles provide a content warning at the beginning of an article and, if possible, indicate which sections of the article readers may need to skip. There have been significant debates about including content warnings in course syllabi in the United States, but I believe content warnings are an integral part of choice because they are a necessary accommodation for many people.

Notably content warnings have been opposed because of: (1) social concerns that they will encourage students to identify as victims and discourage learning about difficult topics and diverse viewpoints, (2) topics for content warnings "are aimed more at women than men (e.g., sexual assault), and this makes such warnings a form of benevolent sexism based on the assumption that women need protection," (3) critiques of political correctness going too far, (4) content warnings are not considered a disability accommodation that professors should have to comply with, and (5) content warnings are seen as "unproductive" because "their use encourages the avoidance of distressing stimuli, and this avoidance behavior is linked to the development, not the prevention, of PTSD symptoms" (Boyson et al., 2018, p. 71–72). Reason 5 is especially problematic because it assumes professors have the right to determine when and how people living with trauma do exposure therapy. "Exposure therapies are designed for clients to remember these traumatic occurrences within a safe environment and to report on them to therapists. This approach does not work for severely traumatized people due to the fact that they are unable to tolerate the exposure" (Härle, 2017, p. 17). Furthermore, content warnings are often misunderstood as censorship, or being requested because people are uncomfortable, rather than recognized as a disability accommodation (Boyson et al., 2018, pp. 71–72; Byron, 2017). People in leadership roles such as professors may also be in need of content warnings or disclosures (Carter, 2015; Kafer, 2016, p. 16). E. A. Lockhart succinctly explains that content/trigger warnings

> are part of an ongoing societal effort to increase the inclusion of people with mental disabilities and trauma, and to increase the overall diversity of the college classroom [. . .] It has been said— repeatedly—that the current generation of college students cannot handle the real world, and that trigger warnings have contributed to this incapacity. I suggest instead that it is the world that cannot handle today's college students, and that trigger warnings are an important tool to facilitate student participation and learning. (2016, pp. 67–68)

Similarly, content warnings are an important accommodation that facilitates vegans participating in their own communities, CAS, Ecoability, and academia in general.

Finally, it is also crucial to be willing to have discussions about what counts as violent or triggering. A basic understanding of content warning suggests that they should only be given for graphic violence, but I will provide several examples that illustrate the complexity of this topic. A large vegan organization approached our vegan university student club several times and requested we hand out their vegan flyers on specific dates. The organization assured me that their flyers did not contain any graphic content, and we did not need to put warning labels on them. I opened the pamphlet to check for myself and remember numbly thinking "I guess they didn't catch it all." I quickly shut the pamphlet, but its images remained. In an emotionally complex example the film *Grizzly Man* describes Timothy Treadwell's life around wild grizzly bears and how he was ultimately *killed by a grizzly bear* (Herzog, 2015). *The film shows no violent footage, but there is a haunting scene where a close friend listens to an audio recording of Timothy's death.* The power of the scene is in how it alludes to violence that is both invisible but hangs heavy in the air. I strongly encourage vegans and CAS scholars to be generous in what they consider to be triggering content. I understand for many people who are not personally triggered, it is difficult to identify triggers and mistakes happen. For others of us it will be more apparent. Furthermore, the potential list of triggers is endless. It is impossible to correctly trigger warn for everything. Perfection is not the point. Attempting to use content warnings appropriately and discussing boundary issues around violence, suffering, and pain strengthen our communities.

Students Against Sexual Assault suggest being respectful and intentional about the language and imagery used in educational and consciousness-raising settings (2018). To this I add that a good practice is to ask honestly: Is this content meant to shock or depict violence, suffering, or pain in its many forms? Could this remind someone of an oppression or abuse that they or someone they know has faced? If the answer is yes to any of these, it may be a good idea to add a content warning. The executive members of our student club Feminists for Animal Liberation decided to tell passing university students that they could buy a cookie and the money would be donated to an animal sanctuary or they could have the cookie for free if they watched a short video. We gave a verbal content warning by explaining that the video showed what happened to cows on a humane milk farm, and that even though it was called humane, what they saw would look like animal abuse. Many students watched the video and others discussed it without watching it. Content warnings can be used creatively to open up dialogue. The vegan program Challenge 22 regularly uses content warnings that maintain an accessible balance by: (1) indicating the following descriptions about how veal, eggs, etc., are made may be hard to read and no one is obligated to read them, and (2) emphasizing that the information is important and they strongly advise people to educate themselves to understand how nonhuman animals are treated and strengthen their commitment to veganism (Challenge 22, personal communication, April 23, 2020).

Conclusion

I agree with Treleaven that "it's our responsibility to adapt mindfulness to meet the specific needs of trauma survivors as opposed to expecting them to adapt to us" and believe this responsibility extends to vegan activist and CAS communities (2018, p. xxii). The impact of violence lingers and for many individuals it cannot be ignored. It also should not be ignored. As Ang writes, "the level of violence involved in the meat, dairy, egg, and other industries that use animals can be quite extreme, and it's only natural if you've felt upset or even traumatized by it" (2016). Recognizing vegans with STSD strengthens the vegan community as a whole by creating access for more individuals, taking violence that human and nonhuman animals face seriously, and challenging systemic oppression. An intersectional and interspecies approach to activism responds to the trauma nonhuman animals may develop from human-caused violence, the trauma humans may already have from their own life experiences, and the trauma humans may develop through witnessing violence against others. I encourage future activism and research on these intersections under the label of Trauma-Informed Activism and other terms.

Acknowledgments

Thank you to my colleagues, friends, and family for their continual encouragement of my activism and academic endeavors. Special thanks to Dr. Leesa K. Fawcett for support with this chapter.

References

Ang, J. (2016, March 9). *Coping with animal cruelty trauma*. In Defense of animals. https://www.idausa.org/coping-animal-cruelty-trauma/

Berger, J. (2004). Trauma without disability, disability without trauma: A disciplinary divide. *JAC, 24*(3), 563–582. https://www-jstor-org.ezproxy.library.yorku.ca/stable/20866643

Boyson, G. A., Prieto, L. R., Holmes, J. D., Landrum, R. E., Miller, R. L., Kujawski Taylor, A., White, J. N., & Kaiser, D. J. (2018). Trigger warnings in psychology classes: What do students think? *Scholarship of Teaching and Learning in Psychology, 4*(2), 69–80. https://doi-org.ezproxy.library.yorku.ca/10.1037/stl0000106

Byron, K. (2017). From infantilizing to world making: Safe spaces and trigger warnings on campus. *Family Relations: Interdisciplinary Journal of Applied Family Science, 66*(1), 116–125. https://doi-org.ezproxy.library.yorku.ca/10.1111/fare.12233

Callie & Nichole. (Podcast Hosts). (2016, September 6). Trigger warnings and veganism (No. 87). [Audio podcast episode]. In *Vegan Warrior Princesses Attack! (the issues)*. http://veganwarriorprincessesattack.com/087-trigger-warnings-and-veganism/

Carter, A. M. (2015). Teaching with trauma: Trigger warnings, feminism, and disability pedagogy. *Disability Studies Quarterly, 35*(2), 9. https://dsq-sds.org/article/view/4652/3935

Caruth, C. (1996). *Unclaimed experience: Trauma, narrative, and history*. The John Hopkins University Press.

Chaudhri, S., Zweig, K. C., Hebbar, P., Angell, S., & Vasan, A. (2019). Trauma-informed care: A strategy to improve primary healthcare engagement for persons with criminal justice system involvement. *Journal of General Internal Medicine, 34*(6), 1048–1052. https://doi-org.ezproxy.library.yorku.ca/10.1007/s11606-018-4783-1

Cole, M. (2014). 'The Greatest Cause on Earth': The historical formation of veganism as an ethical practice. In N. Taylor & R. Twine (Eds.), *The rise of critical animal studies: From the margins to the centre* (pp. 203–224). Routledge.

DeCandia, C. J., & Guarino, K. (2015). Trauma-informed care: An ecological response. *Journal of Child and Youth Care Work*, 25, 7–32. https://www.air.org/sites/default/files/downloads/report/Trauma-Informed-Care-An-Ecological-Response-Guarino-2015.pdf

Diamond, D., Roth, T. L., Fleshner, M., & Zoladz, P. R. (2012). Animal model of PTSD based on clinically relevant features of trauma susceptibility and expression. *European Journal of Psychotraumatology*, 3, 1–37. https://doi-org.ezproxy.library.yorku.ca/10.3402/ejpt.v3i0.19601

Ebenezer, P. K., Wilson, C. B., Wilson, L. D., Nair, A. R., & Francis, J. (2016). The anti-inflammatory effects of blueberries in an animal model of Post-Traumatic Stress Disorder (PTSD). *PLoS ONE*, 11(9), 1–17. https://doi-org.ezproxy.library.yorku.ca/10.1371/journal.pone.0160923

Forner, C. C. (2017). *Dissociation, mindfulness, and creative meditations: Trauma-informed practices to facilitate growth.* Routledge.

Goodman, L., & Bradshaw, G. (2015). Advocating for the souls of animals | an interview with gay bradshaw. *The MOON Magazine*, 3, 1–3. souls-animals-interview-gay-bradshaw-2015-01-03/

Härle, D. (2017). *Trauma-sensitive yoga.* (C. M. Grimm, Trans.). Singing Dragon. (Original work published 2015).

Harper, A. B. (2010). *Sistah vegan: Food, identity, health and society. Black female vegans speak.* Lantern Books.

Herman, J. (2015). *Trauma and recovery: The aftermath of violence—from domestic abuse to political terror* (2015 ed.). Basic Books.

Herzog, W. (Director). (2015). *Grizzly Man* [Film]. Discovery Docs.

Hyland, P., Shevlin, M., Fyvie, C., & Karatzias, T. (2018). Posttraumatic stress disorder and complex posttraumatic stress disorder in DSM-5 and ICD-11: Clinical and behavioral correlates. *Journal of Traumatic Stress*, 31(2), 174–180. https://doi-org.ezproxy.library.yorku.ca/10.1002/jts.22272

Joy, M. [posted by VeganKanal]. (2015, September 13). *Sustainable vegan activism: How to be more effective while advocating for animal rights.* [Video]. Youtube. https://www.youtube.com/watch?v=36XFiTY3SAo&feature=youtu.be

Kafer, A. (2016). Un/Safe disclosures: Scenes of disability and trauma. *Journal of Literary & Cultural Disability Studies*, 10(1), 1–20. https://muse-jhu-edu.ezproxy.library.yorku.ca/article/611309

LaCapra, D. (2016). Trauma, history, memory, identity: what remains? *History and Theory*, 55, 375–400. https://doi-org.ezproxy.library.yorku.ca/10.1111/hith.10817

Lockhart, E. A. (2016). Why trigger warnings are beneficial, perhaps even necessary. *First Amendment Studies*, 50(2), 59–69. https://doiorg.ezproxy.library.yorku.ca/10.1080/21689725.2016.1232623

Mann, C. (2014, August 27). *What strategies help vegans manage their trauma?* Vegan psychologist. https://www.veganpsychologist.com/what-strategies-help-vegans-manage-their-trauma/

Muskett, C. (2014). Trauma-informed care in inpatient mental health settings: A review of the literature. *International Journal of Mental Health Nursing*, *23*(1), 51–59. https://doi-org.ezproxy.library.yorku.ca/10.1111/inm.12012

Nibert, D. (2014). Animals, immigrants, and profits: Slaughterhouses and the political economy of oppression. In J. Sorenson (Ed.), *Critical animal studies: Thinking the unthinkable*. Canadian Scholars' Press.

Nimmo, A., & Huggard P. (2013). A systematic review of the measurement of compassion fatigue, vicarious trauma, and secondary traumatic stress in physicians. *Australasian Journal of Disaster and Trauma Studies*, *2013–1*, 37–44. https://www.massey.ac.nz/~trauma/issues/2013-1/AJDTS_2013-1_Nimmo.pdf

Nocella II, A. J. (2012). Defining eco-ability: Social justice and the intersectionality of disability, nonhuman animals, and ecology. In A. J. Nocella II, J. K. C. Bentley, & J. M. Duncan (Eds.), *Earth, animal, and disability liberation: The rise of the eco-ability movement* (pp. 3–21). Peter Lang Publishing.

Nocella II, A. J., Bentley, J. K. C., & Duncan, J. M. (Eds.). (2012). Introduction: The rise of eco-ability. *Earth, animal, and disability liberation: The rise of the eco-ability movement.* (pp. xiii–xxii). Peter Lang Publishing.

Nocella II, A., Sorenson, J., Socha, K., & Matsuoko, A. (2014). *Defining critical animal studies: An intersectional social justice approach for liberation.* Peter Lang Publishing.

Phillips, J. (2015). PTSD in DSM-5: Understanding the changes. *Psychiatric Times*, *32*(9), n.p. https://www.psychiatrictimes.com/ptsd/ptsd-dsm-5-understanding-changes

Schlote, S. (2015, May 15). *Trauma-sensitive mindfulness, meditation and yoga.* Canadian Counselling and Psychotherapy Association. https://www.ccpa-accp.ca/wp-content/uploads/2015/11/2015conf.Trauma-SensitiveMindfulness.pdf

Sorenson, J. (2014). *Critical animal studies: Thinking the unthinkable.* Canadian Scholars' Press Inc.

Stam, R. (2007). PTSD and stress sensitisation: A tale of brain and body part 2: Animal models. *Neuroscience and Biobehavioral Reviews*, *31*(4), 558–584. https://doi-org.ezproxy.library.yorku.ca/10.1016/j.neubiorev.2007.01.001

Students Against Sexual Assault (2016, November 7). *Creating trauma-informed activist spaces: A workshop by SASA.* Facebook. https://www.facebook.com/events/277295712788265/

Students Against Sexual Assault (2017, March 6). *Trauma informed activism workshop.* Facebook. https://www.facebook.com/events/campus-center-103104/trauma-informed-activism-workshop/1175622965868853/

Students Against Sexual Assault (2018, November 8). *Trauma informed activism workshop.* Facebook. https://www.facebook.com/events/277295712788265/

Taft, C. (2016, March 19). *Trauma in animal advocacy.* Vegan Publishers. http://vegan-publishers.com/trauma/

The Canadian CED Network. (2020, February 20). *Healing for change: Trauma-informed activism.* The Canadian CED Network. https://ccednetrcdec.ca/en/event/2020/02/20/healing-change-trauma-informed-activism

The Vegan Society. (n.d.). *History*. The Vegan Society. https://www.vegansociety.com/about-us/history

Treleaven, D. A. (2018). *Trauma-sensitive mindfulness: Practices for safe and transformative healing*. W.W. Norton Company.

van Dernoot Lipsky, L., & Burk C. (2009). *Trauma stewardship: An everyday guide to caring `for self while caring for others*. Berrett-Koehler Publishers, Inc.

Way, I., Vandeusen, K. M., Martin, G., Applegate, B., & Jandle, D. (2004). Vicarious trauma: A comparison of clinicians who treat survivors of sexual abuse and sexual offenders. *Journal of Interpersonal Violence, 19*(1), 49–71. https://doi-org.ezproxy.library.yorku.ca/10.1177/0886260503259050

Wrenn, C. L. (2014, January 8). *Graphic animal suffering, secondary PTSD, and abolitionism*. The Academic Activist Vegan. http://academicactivistvegan.blogspot.com/2014/01/graphic-animal-suffering-secondary-ptsd.html

Afterword

I suppose most everyone these days uses social media as a temporary distraction and reprieve from everyday tasks. Recently I was scrolling through Twitter and became enamored of a touching video clip depicting a dog who appears to be a Boxer mix helping another dog, a Beagle mix who is blind, down a flight of stairs: https://www.youtube.com/watch?v=xya76LFhxvc The video has been edited to include music, "Just The Two of Us" by Bill Withers. This video struck a chord with viewers around the globe on multiple platforms, and rightly so. Altruism is one of the most gratifying acts we can witness.

Meanwhile, two days ago I was taking my dog Amalee, an 11–12-year-old rescue Pitbull-Daschund mix and domestic violence refugee whom I consider to be a soul mate, to our neighborhood dog park. As she explored and played, a young man and his dog entered the far end of the park. The dog, a black and white spotted spaniel mix, was learning to walk on three legs, and appeared to be a recent amputee still adapting to being a bit off-balance. Amalee marched right up and plowed into this new arrival, quickly putting her on her back in submission. I apologized to the dog's person; he said she had been spending a lot of time on her back recently anyway—I assume in recovery. Sadly, Amalee's history with disability is typified by this encounter. I've seen her overturn a pug whose back legs required a cart due to immobility, repeatedly hump a senior pug who was blind, and I've caught her in the window barking ferociously at a visually impaired child across the street learning to use a cane. She once started barking at a gentleman in a wheelchair with cerebral palsy who wanted to pet her at a festival. She seems uncertain and a little afraid (judging by the way the hair rises on her back) of physical differences or erratic movements that deviate from her norms. Her apprehension includes both dogs and humans as I have observed Amalee reacting this way during the decade she has been with my family. This is challenging, and often mortifying for me as her human companion. Still, I strive to redirect her behavior and swiftly remove her from inflicting harm with a compassionate understanding that I cannot know what it's like to be her. She has shown me, through her demeanor, what some of her trauma must have been. When we brought her home from the county shelter, she was afraid of lamp cords and would routinely march up to dark-haired bearded men in baseball caps and start barking at them, including my brother. Now she eagerly prances up to strangers with her tail wagging, fully expecting to meet a friend. Each milestone in her comfort and trust suggests she is eclipsing her past, one lived experience at a time.

As this transformational book so aptly demonstrates, when it comes to disability, we humans are subject to the same foibles and shortcomings as my beloved dog. But unlike her, we are not excusably innocent in this collective character flaw which spans the gamut of ignorance to bigotry. Certainly, within any social justice movement one would want to cultivate a culture of liberation, inclusion, affirmation, and celebration of diverse identities. One would hope veganism could be free of oppressive "isms," such as ableism, racism, sexism, and speciesism. This book sheds light on the ways our demeanor toward the perceived "other," including human and nonhuman animals, has fallen short and continues to falter. It gives us a clear direction within the vegan movement to ally our resources, elevate our consciousness, and push forward through critical rhetorical activism, ecoability equity, the ethics of care, queer ecology, and trauma informed activism into a more evolved version of who we really are.

In Amalee's case, the only exception to her pattern of discomfort with disability is when a member of her own pack (whether dog or human) becomes injured and incapacitated. In these instances, such as when her adopted brother Beckham, a death-row rescue Pitbull, needed surgery, she hovered close by, offering comfort and concern. I suffer from migraines, and she becomes so attentive to me at the apex of pain that she places her body against mine for days at a time, scarcely leaving except to drink, eat, and relieve herself. She is the greatest healer I have ever known.

As with all forms of prejudice, it is easier to get past the limitations of fear when you know someone, and this seems equally true for Amalee and we humans. We need to recognize that we don't have to "know" another in the sense of having a personal connection or relationship in order to *know* them; we must reawaken to our common humanity and our interspeciesim.

We must begin to realize that separation is—and always was—an illusion. These movements—disability, animal, and environmental rights—steeped in the powerful mix of compassion and justice known as ecoability—have given us the foundation to fuse our endeavors and rise united, "Just the Three of Us."

Contributors' Biographies

Amber E. George, Ph.D., is Assistant Professor at Galen College where she teaches courses in philosophy, sociology, and cultural studies. Dr. George co-edited the book, *The Image of Disability: Essays on Media Representations*; *Screening the Non/Human: Representations of Animal Others in the Media*; and *The Intersectionality of Critical Animal, Disability, and Environmental Studies*. She is the current editor of the *Journal for Critical Animal Studies (JCAS)*, has served as an editor on several projects for the *Advocacy and Systems Change Journal*, and is on the review board of *Green Theory and Praxis Journal* and *Transformative Justice Book Series*.

Lea Lani Kinikini, received her doctorate from University of Auckland, New Zealand, masters from University of Hawai'i, and bachelors from University of Utah. She is a researcher and educational practitioner who has worked internationally in Hawai'i, New Zealand, Oceania, and now Salt Lake County. Her research has examined the school to prison to deportation pipeline with a focus on case law and Pacific Islander youth gangs. She has conceptualized how legal fictions are extrapolated both in the public sphere and in the legal realm to produce ranked or "marked" populations underlined by racial classes. She currently is Chief Diversity Officer at Salt Lake Community College working on building solutions to over-incarceration and is committed to creating equity through educational justice innovations.

Rebecca Eli Long is an MA candidate in Appalachian Studies at Appalachian State University in Boone, North Carolina. Their research examines the role that disability has played throughout Appalachian social movements, both past and present. Trained as an applied anthropologist, Rebecca Eli's research spans multiple academic disciplines with a focus on creating a just, sustainable future. They are also a leader in disability justice organizing on their campus and president of the Autistic Students and Allies of the High Country, where they focus on supporting neurodiversity in higher education.

Z. Zane McNeill is a dirt queer from Appalachia fighting for y'all to really mean all. They are a genderqueer activist-scholar, socially engaged artist, and 10-year vegan passionate about consistent anti-oppression work that uplifts the most marginalized within our communities. He is the editor of the collection, *Vegan Entanglements: Dismantling Racial and Carceral Capitalism.* .

S. Marek Muller is Assistant Professor of Rhetorical Studies at Florida Atlantic University. Her work is at the nexus of environmental communication, critical intercultural communication, and rhetorical studies. Specifically, she is interested in the rhetorical constructions of "humanity" and "animality" as they are used in the service of human and nonhuman animal oppression and liberation.

Anthony J. Nocella II, Ph.D., is Assistant Professor in the Department of Criminal Justice and Criminology in the Institute of Public Safety at Salt Lake Community College. He is the editor of the *Peace Studies Journal, Transformative Justice Journal,* and co-editor of five-book series including *Critical Animal Studies and Theory* with Lexington Books and *Hip Hop Studies and Activism* with Peter Lang Publishing. He is National Director of Save the Kids and Executive Director of the Institute for Critical Animal Studies. He has published over fifty book chapters or articles and forty books. He has been interviewed by New York Times, Washington Post, Houston Chronicles, Fresno Bee, Fox, CBS, CNN, C-SPAN, and Los Angeles Times.

T.N. Rowan is a PhD student in the Faculty of Environmental Studies at York University. They are currently researching world building and its potential as an environmental ethics methodology and form of arts-based research. T.N. Rowan is proposing world building that can facilitate intersectional activist communities and individuals in identifying and responding to issues that matter to them. They frame world building as an accessible and creative form of critical thinking. T.N. Rowan's research interests also include naming, identity, violence, and trauma across a variety of boundaries including species, gender, and sexual orientation.

Daniel Salomon is a doctorate student in Urban Studies at Portland State University. An MA in Theological Research from Andover Newton

Theological School with Graduate Certificate in Science and Religion from Boston Theological Institute, as well as a BS Cum Laude from Salisbury University (with concentrations in Biology, Environmental Studies and Conflict Analysis/Dispute Resolution) and a Naturalist Certificate from the Au Sable Institute of Environmental Studies. Salomon is the author of seven books on the environment and a contributor to the ecoability field. Salomon's latest book *God's Kindness* was reviewed by Ed Langlois in the Catholic Sentinel of the Portland Oregon Archdioceses. Salomon lives in Portland Oregon and is a lifelong vegetarian.

Clifton G. Sanders, received his doctorate from University of Utah and his bachelors from Hamline University. Sanders is the Provost for Academic Affairs at Salt Lake Community College. He has more than 25 years teaching, administrative and leadership experience in higher education. He led the development of several STEM programs and is a collaborator on several local, regional, and national initiatives on education, diversity and inclusivity, and workforce development. His scientific work resulted in six patents in biomaterials technology. He is a University of Utah Chemistry Department Distinguished Alumnus, and he coauthored a 2009 paper on music and democracy published in *Radical Philosophy Review.*

Alaina Sigler has a Master of Education in Literacy Education from the University of Cincinnati. Her passions are writing, Critical Animal Studies, and volunteering at a local farmed animal sanctuary. She has organized for nonhuman animals since 2014 around the Denver, Colorado area. She lives with a rescued dog named Meeka.

Elisa Stone, English Professor, helped create Salt Lake Community College's Gender & Sexuality Student Resource Center and helps plan the Utah Pride Center's gender-evolution conference. Via SLCC's Beloved Community Project, Elisa co-educates students about Martin Luther King, Jr. She received SLCC's Unsung Sheroes Award, President's Inclusivity & Equity Award, and Utah Campus Compact's Engaged Faculty Award. Elisa's SLCC Community Writing Center Teens Write Mentoring Program won Innovation of the Year and National Bellwether Finalist. Joining an anti-stigma campaign for the Desmond Tutu HIV Foundation, Elisa connected with Nobel Peace Prize winner Tutu following his Peace with Justice Award in Cape Town, South Africa.

Birkan Taş is a postdoctoral researcher and lecturer at the University of Kassel, Germany. He holds a BA in Psychology from Boğaziçi University in

Istanbul and an MA in Cultural Studies from Istanbul Bilgi University. He completed his PhD thesis at the Amsterdam School for Cultural Analysis (University of Amsterdam) in 2016. His research interests encompass theories of gender and sexuality, the politics of temporality in disability and queer theory, and human-animal interaction. Currently he is working on an interdisciplinary project on assistance dogs.

Index

RADICAL ANIMAL STUDIES AND TOTAL LIBERATION

Anthony J. Nocella II, SERIES EDITOR

The **Radical Animal Studies and Total Liberation** book series branches out of Critical Animal Studies (a field co-founded by Anthony J. Nocella II) with the argument that criticism is not enough. Action must follow theory. This series demands that scholars are engaged with their subjects both theoretically and actively via radical, revolutionary, intersectional action for total liberation. Founded in anarchism, the series provides space for scholar-activists who challenge authoritarianism and oppression in their many daily forms. **Radical Animal Studies and Total Liberation** promotes accessible and inclusive scholarship that is based on personal narrative as well as traditional research, and is especially interested in the advancement of interwoven voices and perspectives from multiple radical, revolutionary social justice groups and movements such as Black Lives Matter, Idle No More, Earth First!, the Zapatistas, ADAPT, prison abolition, LGBTTQQIA rights, disability liberation, Earth Liberation Front, Animal Liberation Front, political prisoners, radical transnational feminism, environmental justice, food justice, youth justice, and Hip Hop activism.

To order other books in this series please contact our Customer Service Department:

PETERLANG@PRESSWAREHOUSE.COM (WITHIN THE U.S.)

ORDERS@PETERLANG.COM (OUTSIDE THE U.S.)

To find out more about the series or browse a full list of titles, please visit our website:

WWW.PETERLANG.COM

www.ingramcontent.com/pod-product-compliance
Lightning Source LLC
Chambersburg PA
CBHW050616280326
41932CB00016B/3073